Getting Started with Amazon Redshift

Enter the exciting world of Amazon Redshift for big data, cloud computing, and scalable data warehousing

Stefan Bauer

PUBLISHING

BIRMINGHAM - MUMBAI

Getting Started with Amazon Redshift

Copyright © 2013 Packt Publishing

All rights reserved. No part of this book may be reproduced, stored in a retrieval system, or transmitted in any form or by any means, without the prior written permission of the publisher, except in the case of brief quotations embedded in critical articles or reviews.

Every effort has been made in the preparation of this book to ensure the accuracy of the information presented. However, the information contained in this book is sold without warranty, either express or implied. Neither the author, nor Packt Publishing, and its dealers and distributors will be held liable for any damages caused or alleged to be caused directly or indirectly by this book.

Packt Publishing has endeavored to provide trademark information about all of the companies and products mentioned in this book by the appropriate use of capitals. However, Packt Publishing cannot guarantee the accuracy of this information.

First published: June 2013

Production Reference: 2100613

Published by Packt Publishing Ltd.
Livery Place
35 Livery Street
Birmingham B3 2PB, UK.

ISBN 978-1-78217-808-8

www.packtpub.com

Cover Image by Suresh Mogre (suresh.mogre.99@gmail.com)

Credits

Author
Stefan Bauer

Reviewers
Koichi Fujikawa

Matthew Luu

Masashi Miyazaki

Acquisition Editors
Antony Lowe

Erol Staveley

Commissioning Editor
Sruthi Kutty

Technical Editors
Dennis John

Dominic Pereira

Copy Editors
Insiya Morbiwala

Alfida Paiva

Project Coordinator
Sneha Modi

Proofreader
Maria Gould

Indexer
Tejal Soni

Graphics
Abhinash Sahu

Production Coordinator
Pooja Chiplunkar

Cover Work
Pooja Chiplunkar

About the Author

Stefan Bauer has worked in business intelligence and data warehousing since the late 1990s on a variety of platforms in a variety of industries. Stefan has worked with most major databases, including Oracle, Informix, SQL Server, and Amazon Redshift as well as other data storage models, such as Hadoop. Stefan provides insight into hardware architecture, database modeling, as well as developing in a variety of ETL and BI tools, including Integration Services, Informatica, Analysis Services, Reporting Services, Pentaho, and others. In addition to traditional development, Stefan enjoys teaching topics on architecture, database administration, and performance tuning. Redshift is a natural extension fit for Stefan's broad understanding of database technologies and how they relate to building enterprise-class data warehouses.

I would like to thank everyone who had a hand in pushing me along in the writing of this book, but most of all, my wife Jodi for the incredible support in making this project possible.

About the Reviewers

Koichi Fujikawa is a co-founder of Hapyrus a company providing web services that help users to make their big data more valuable on the cloud, and is currently focusing on Amazon Redshift. This company is also an official partner of Amazon Redshift and presents technical solutions to the world.

He has over 12 years of experience as a software engineer and an entrepreneur in the U.S. and Japan.

> To review this book, I thank our colleagues in Hapyrus Inc., Lawrence Gryseels and Britt Sanders. Without cooperation from our family, we could not have finished reviewing this book.

Matthew Luu is a recent graduate of the University of California, Santa Cruz. He started working at Hapyrus and has quickly learned all about Amazon Redshift.

> I would like to thank my family and friends who continue to support me in all that I do. I would also like to thank the team at Hapyrus for the essential skills they have taught me.

Masashi Miyazaki is a software engineer of Hapyrus Inc. He has been focusing on Amazon Redshift since the end of 2012, and has been developing a web application and Fluent plugins for Hapyrus's FlyData service.

His background is in the Java-based messaging middleware for mission critical systems, iOS application for iPhone and iPad, and Ruby scripting.

His URL address is `http://mmasashi.jp/`.

www.PacktPub.com

Support files, eBooks, discount offers and more

You might want to visit www.PacktPub.com for support files and downloads related to your book.

Did you know that Packt offers eBook versions of every book published, with PDF and ePub files available? You can upgrade to the eBook version at www.PacktPub.com and as a print book customer, you are entitled to a discount on the eBook copy. Get in touch with us at service@packtpub.com for more details.

At www.PacktPub.com, you can also read a collection of free technical articles, sign up for a range of free newsletters and receive exclusive discounts and offers on Packt books and eBooks.

http://PacktLib.PacktPub.com

Do you need instant solutions to your IT questions? PacktLib is Packt's online digital book library. Here, you can access, read and search across Packt's entire library of books.

Why Subscribe?
- Fully searchable across every book published by Packt
- Copy and paste, print and bookmark content
- On demand and accessible via web browser

Free Access for Packt account holders

If you have an account with Packt at www.PacktPub.com, you can use this to access PacktLib today and view nine entirely free books. Simply use your login credentials for immediate access.

Instant Updates on New Packt Books

Get notified! Find out when new books are published by following @PacktEnterprise on Twitter, or the *Packt Enterprise* Facebook page.

Table of Contents

Preface

Data warehousing as an industry has been around for quite a number of years now. There have been many evolutions in data modeling, storage, and ultimately the vast variety of tools that the business user now has available to help utilize their quickly growing stores of data. As the industry is moving more towards self service business intelligence solutions for the business user, there are also changes in how data is being stored. Amazon Redshift is one of those "game-changing" changes that is not only driving down the total cost, but also driving up the ability to store even more data to enable even better business decisions to be made. This book will not only help you get started in the traditional "how-to" sense, but also provide background and understanding to enable you to make the best use of the data that you already have.

What this book covers

Chapter 1, *Overview*, takes an in-depth look at what we will be covering in the book, as well as a look at what Redshift provides at the current Amazon pricing levels.

Chapter 2, *Transition to Redshift*, provides the details necessary to start your Redshift cluster. We will begin to look at the tools you will use to connect, as well as the kinds of features that are and are not supported in Redshift.

Chapter 3, *Loading Your Data to Redshift*, will takes you through the steps of creating tables, and the steps necessary to get data loaded into the database.

Chapter 4, *Managing Your Data*, provides you with a good understanding of the day-to-day operation of a Redshift cluster. Everything from backup and recover, to managing user queries with Workload Management is covered here.

Chapter 5, *Querying Data*, gives you the details you need to understand how to monitor the queries you have running, and also helps you to understand explain plans. We will also look at the things you will need to convert your existing queries to Redshift.

Chapter 6, Best Practices, will tie together the remaining details about monitoring your Redshift cluster, and provides some guidance on general best practices to get you started in the right direction.

Appendix, Reference Materials, will provide you with a point of reference for terms, important commands, and system tables. There is also a consolidated list of links for software, and other utilities discussed in the book.

What you need for this book

In order to work with the examples, and run your own Amazon Redshift cluster, there are a few things you will need, which are as follows:.

- An Amazon Web Services account with permissions to create and manage Redshift
- Software and drivers (links in the *Appendix, Reference Materials*)
- Client JDBC drivers
- Client ODBC drivers (optional)
- An Amazon S3 file management utility (such as Cloudberry Explorer)
- Query software (such as EMS SQL Manager)
- An Amazon EC2 instance (optional) for the command-line interface

Who this book is for

This book is intended to provide a practical as well as a technical overview for everyone who is interested in this technology. There is something here for everyone interested in this technology. The CIOs will gain an understanding of what their technical staff is talking about, and the technical implementation personnel will get an in-depth view of the technology and what it will take to implement their own solutions.

Conventions

In this book, you will find a number of styles of text that distinguish between different kinds of information. Here are some examples of these styles, and an explanation of their meaning.

Code words in text, database table names, folder names, filenames, file extensions, pathnames, dummy URLs, user input, and Twitter handles are shown as follows: "We can include other contexts through the use of the `include` directive."

A block of code is set as follows:

```
CREATE TABLE census_data
    (
        fips                    VARCHAR(10),
        pop_estimate            BIGINT,
        pop_estimate_base       BIGINT,
        pop_estimate_chg        DECIMAL(5, 1),
        pop_total               BIGINT
    . . .
```

When we wish to draw your attention to a particular part of a code block, the relevant lines or items are set in bold:

```
CREATE TABLE census_data
    (
        fips                    VARCHAR(10),
        pop_estimate            BIGINT,
        pop_estimate_base       BIGINT,
        pop_estimate_chg        DECIMAL(5, 1),
        pop_total               BIGINT
    . . .
```

Any command-line input or output is written as follows:

```
# cexport AWS_CONFIG_FILE=/home/user/cliconfig.txt
```

New terms and **important words** are shown in bold. Words that you see on the screen, in menus or dialog boxes for example, appear in the text like this: "Launch the cluster creation wizard by selecting the **Launch Cluster** option from the Amazon Redshift Management console."

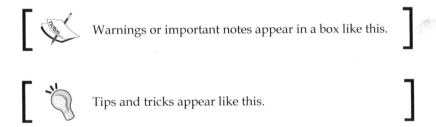

Warnings or important notes appear in a box like this.

Tips and tricks appear like this.

Reader feedback

Feedback from our readers is always welcome. Let us know what you think about this book—what you liked or may have disliked. Reader feedback is important for us to develop titles that you really get the most out of.

To send us general feedback, simply send an e-mail to feedback@packtpub.com, and mention the book title via the subject of your message.

If there is a topic that you have expertise in and you are interested in either writing or contributing to a book, see our author guide on www.packtpub.com/authors.

Customer support

Now that you are the proud owner of a Packt book, we have a number of things to help you to get the most from your purchase.

Downloading the example code

You can download the example code files for all Packt books you have purchased from your account at http://www.packtpub.com. If you purchased this book elsewhere, you can visit http://www.packtpub.com/support and register to have the files e-mailed directly to you.

Errata

Although we have taken every care to ensure the accuracy of our content, mistakes do happen. If you find a mistake in one of our books—maybe a mistake in the text or the code—we would be grateful if you would report this to us. By doing so, you can save other readers from frustration and help us improve subsequent versions of this book. If you find any errata, please report them by visiting http://www.packtpub.com/submit-errata, selecting your book, clicking on the **errata submission form** link, and entering the details of your errata. Once your errata are verified, your submission will be accepted and the errata will be uploaded on our website, or added to any list of existing errata, under the Errata section of that title. Any existing errata can be viewed by selecting your title from http://www.packtpub.com/support.

Piracy

Piracy of copyright material on the Internet is an ongoing problem across all media. At Packt, we take the protection of our copyright and licenses very seriously. If you come across any illegal copies of our works, in any form, on the Internet, please provide us with the location address or website name immediately so that we can pursue a remedy.

Please contact us at copyright@packtpub.com with a link to the suspected pirated material.

We appreciate your help in protecting our authors, and our ability to bring you valuable content.

Questions

You can contact us at questions@packtpub.com if you are having a problem with any aspect of the book, and we will do our best to address it.

1
Overview

In this chapter, we will take an in-depth look at the topics we will be covering throughout the book. This chapter will also give you some background as to why Redshift is different from other databases you have used in the past, as well as the general types of things you will need to consider when starting up your first Redshift cluster.

This book, *Getting Started with Amazon Redshift*, is intended to provide a practical as well as technical overview of the product for anyone that may be intrigued as to why this technology is interesting as well as those that actually wish to take it for a test drive. Ideally, there is something here for everyone interested in this technology. The Chief Information Officer (CIO) will gain an understanding of what their technical staff are talking about, while the technical and implementation personnel will get an insight into the technology they need to understand the strengths and limitations of Redshift product. Throughout this book, I will try to relate the examples to things that are understandable and easy to replicate using your own environment. Just to be clear, this book is not a cookbook series on schema design and data warehouse implementation. I will explain some of the data warehouse specifics along the way as they are important to the process; however, this is not a crash course in dimensional modeling or data warehouse design principles.

Redshift is a brand new entry into the market, with the initial preview beta release in November of 2012 and the full version made available for purchase on February 15, 2013. As I will explain in the relevant parts of this book, there have been a few early adoption issues that I experienced along the way. That is not to say it is not a good product. So far I am impressed, very impressed actually, with what I have seen. Performance while I was testing has, been quite good, and when there was an occasional issue, the Redshift technical team's response has been stellar. The performance on a small cluster has been impressive; later, we will take a look at some runtimes and performance metrics. We will look more at the *how* and *why* of the performance that Redshift is achieving. Much of it has to do with how the data is being stored in a columnar data store and the work that has been done to reduce I/O. I know you are on the first chapter of this book and we are already talking about things such as columnar stores and I/O reduction, but don't worry; the book will progress logically, and by the time you get to the best practices at the end, you will be able to understand Redshift in a much better, more complete way. Most importantly, you will have the confidence to go and give it a try.

In the broadest terms, Amazon Redshift could be considered a traditional data warehouse platform, and in reality, although a gross oversimplification, that would not be far from the truth. In fact, Amazon Redshift is intended to be exactly that, only at a price, having scalability that is difficult to beat. You can see the video and documentation published by Amazon that lists the cost at one-tenth the cost of traditional warehousing on the Internet. There are, in my mind, clearly going to be some savings on the hardware side and on some of the human resources necessary to run both the hardware and large-scale databases locally. Don't be under the illusion that all management and maintenance tasks are taken away simply by moving data to a hosted platform; it is still *your* data to manage. The hardware, software patching, and disk management (all of which are no small tasks) have been taken on by Amazon. Disk management, particularly the automated recovery from disk failure, and even the ability to begin querying a cluster that is being restored (even before it is done) are all powerful and compelling things Amazon has done to reduce your workload and increase up-time.

I am sure that by now you are wondering, why Redshift? If you guessed that it is with reference to the term from astronomy and the work that Edwin Hubble did to define the relationship of the astronomical phenomenon known as redshift and the expansion of our universe, you would have guessed correctly. The ability to perform online resizes of your cluster as your data continually expands makes Redshift a very appropriate name for this technology.

> #Amazon #Redshift - Cloud-based Big Data Analytics at 10% the cost of traditional -...

Pricing

As you think about your own ever-expanding universe of data, there are two basic options to choose from: **High Storage Extra Large (XL) DW Node** and **High Storage Eight Extra Large (8XL) DW Node**. As with most Amazon products, there is a menu approach to the pricing. **On-Demand**, as with most of their products, is the most expensive. It currently costs 85 cents per hour per node for the large nodes and $6.80 per hour for the extra-large nodes. The **Reserved** pricing, with some upfront costs, can get you pricing as low as 11 cents per hour for the large nodes. I will get into further specifics on cluster choices in a later section when we discuss the actual creation of the cluster. As you take a look at pricing, recognize that it is a little bit of a moving target. One can assume, based on the track record of just about every product that Amazon has rolled out, that Redshift will also follow the same model of price reductions as efficiencies of scale are realized within Amazon. For example, the **DynamoDB** product recently had another price drop that now makes that service available at 85 percent of the original cost. Given the track record with the other AWS offerings, I would suggest that these prices are really "worst case". With some general understanding that you will gain from this book, the selection of the node type and quantity should become clear to you as you are ready to embark on your own journey with this technology. An important point, however, is that you can see how relatively easily companies that thought an enterprise warehouse was out of their reach can afford a tremendous amount of storage and processing power at what is already a reasonable cost. The current On-Demand pricing from Amazon for Redshift is as follows:

Region: US East (N. Virginia) ▾

DW Node Class (On-Demand)	Hourly
XL Node - 2TB storage (Per Node)	$0.850 per hour
8XL Node - 16TB storage (Per Node)	$6.800 per hour

So, with an upfront commitment, you will have a significant reduction in your hourly per-node pricing, as you can see in the following screenshot:

1 Year Reserved Instance Pricing

Region: US East (N. Virginia) ▾

DW Node Class (Reserved)	1yr Reserved Instance	
	Upfront	Hourly
XL Node - 2TB storage (Per Node)	$2,500	$0.215 per hour
8XL Node - 16TB storage (Per Node)	$20,000	$1.720 per hour

The three-year pricing affords you the best overall value, in that the upfront costs are not significantly more than the one year reserved node and the per hour cost per node is almost half of what the one year price is. For two XL nodes, you can recoup the upfront costs in 75 days over the on-demand pricing and then pay significantly less in the long run. I suggest, unless you truly are just testing, that you purchase the three-year reserved instance.

Region: US East (N. Virginia) ▾	
DW Node Class (On-Demand)	**Hourly**
XL Node - 2TB storage (Per Node)	$0.850 per hour
8XL Node - 16TB storage (Per Node)	$6.800 per hour

Configuration options

As you saw outlined in the pricing information, there are two kinds of nodes you can choose from when creating your cluster.

The basic configuration of the large Redshift (dw.hs1.xlarge) node is as follows:

- CPU: 2 Virtual Cores (Intel Xeon E5)
- Memory: 15 GB
- Storage: 3 HDD with 2 TB of locally attached storage
- Network: Moderate
- Disk I/O: Moderate

The basic configuration of the extra-large Redshift (dw.hs1.8xlarge) node is as follows:

- CPU: 16 Virtual Cores (Intel Xeon E5)
- Memory: 120 GB
- Storage: 24 HDD with 16 TB of locally attached storage
- Network: 10 GB Ethernet
- Disk I/O: Very high

The hs in the naming convention is the designation Amazon has used for high-density storage.

An important point to note; if you are interested in a single-node configuration, the only option you have is the smaller of the two options. The 8XL extra-large nodes are only available in a multi-node configuration. We will look at how data is managed on the nodes and why multiple nodes are important in a later chapter. For production use, we should have at least two nodes. There are performance reasons as well as data protection reasons for this that we will look at later. The large node cluster supports up to 64 nodes for a total capacity of anything between 2 and 128 terabytes of storage. The extra-large node cluster supports from 2 to 100 nodes for a total capacity of anything between 32 terabytes and 1.6 petabytes. For the purpose of discussion, a multi-node configuration with two large instances would have 4 terabytes of storage available and therefore would also have four terabytes of associated backup space. Before we get too far ahead of ourselves, a node is a single host consisting of one of the previous configurations. When I talk about a cluster, it is a collection of one or more nodes that are running together, as seen in the following figure. Each cluster runs an Amazon Redshift database engine.

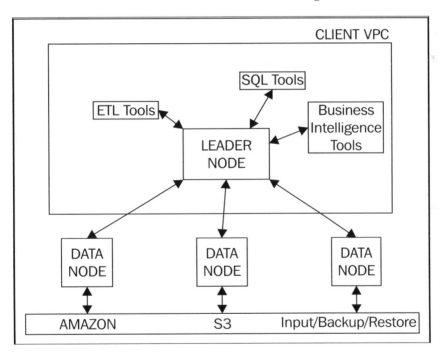

Data storage

As you begin thinking about the kinds of I/O rates you will need to support your installation, you will be surprised (or at least I was) with the kind of throughput you will be able to achieve on a three-drive, 2 TB node. So, before you apply too many of your predefined beliefs, I suggest estimating your total storage needs and picking the node configuration that will best fit your overall storage needs on a reasonably small number of nodes. As I mentioned previously, the extra-large configuration will only start as multi-node so the base configuration for an extra-large configuration is really 32 TB of space. Not a small warehouse by most peoples' standards. If your overall storage needs will ultimately be in the 8 to 10 terabyte range, start with one or two large nodes (the 2 terabyte per node variety). Having more than one node will become important for parallel loading operations as well as for disk mirroring, which I will discuss in later chapters. As you get started, don't feel you need to allocate your total architecture and space requirements right off. Resizing, which we will also cover in detail, is not a difficult operation, and it even allows for resizing between the large and extra-large node configurations. Do note however that you cannot mix different node sizes in a cluster because all the nodes in a single cluster, must be of the same type. You may start with a single node if you wish; I do, however, recommend a minimum of two nodes for performance and data protection reasons. You may consider the extra-large nodes if you have very large data volumes and are adding data at a very fast pace. Otherwise, from a performance perspective, the large nodes have performed very well in all of my testing scenarios.

If you have been working on data warehouse projects for any length of time, this product will cause you to question some of your preconceived ideas of hardware configuration in general. As most data warehouse professionals know, greater speed in a data warehouse is often achieved with improved I/O. For years I have discussed and built presentations specifically on the SAN layout, spindle configuration, and other disk optimizations as ways of improving the overall query performance. The methodology that Amazon has implemented in Redshift is to eliminate a large percentage of that work and to use a relatively small number of directly attached disks. There has been an impressive improvement with these directly attached disks as they eliminate unnecessary I/O operations. With the concept of "zone mapping," there are entire blocks of data that can be skipped in the read operations, as the database knows that the zone is not needed to answer the query. The blocks are also considerably larger than most databases at 1 MB per block. As I have already mentioned, the data is stored in a column store. Think of the **column store** as a physical layout that will allow the reading of a single column from a table without having to read any other part of the row. Traditionally, a row would be placed on disk within a block (or multiple blocks). If you wanted to read all of the **first_name** fields in a given table, you would read them block by block, picking up the **first_ name** column from each of the records as you encountered them.

Think of a vinyl record, in this example, **Data Greatest Hits Vol-1** (refer to the following figure). The needle starts reading the record, and you start listening for **first_name**; so, you will hear **first_name** (remember that), then you will hear **last_name** and **age** (you choose to forget those two, as you are only interested in **first_name**), and then we'll get to the next record and you'll hear **first_name** (remember that), **last_name**, **age** (forget those), and so on.

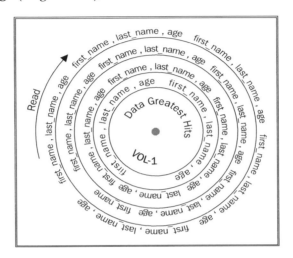

In a column store, you would query the database in the same way, but then you would start reading block by block only those blocks containing the **first_name** data. The album **Data Greatest Hits Vol-2** (refer to the following figure) is now configured differently, and you'll put the needle down on the section of the record for **first_name** and start reading **first_name**, **first_name**, **first_name**, and so on. There was no wasted effort in reading **last_name** and **age** at all.

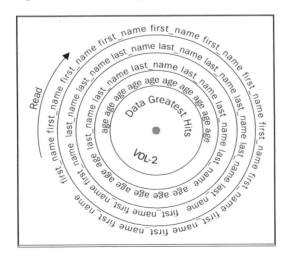

Likewise, if you were reading the **age** column, you would start with the **age** data, ignoring all of the data in the **first_name** and **last_name** columns. Now apply compression (which we will cover later as well) to the blocks. A single targeted read operation of a large 1 MB block will retrieve an incredible amount of usable data. All of this is being done while going massively parallel across all available nodes. I am sure that without even having started your cluster yet, you can get a sense of why this is going to be a different experience from what you are used to.

> For modest-sized (~1B row), highly compressible columnar data, #aws #redshift performance compared to MySQL is nothing short of spectacular.

Considerations for your environment

I will cover only some of the specifics as we'll discuss these topics in other sections; however, as you begin to think about the migration of your data and processes to Redshift, there are a few things to put at the back of your mind now. As you read this book, you will need to to take into consideration the things that are unique to your environment; for example, your current schema design and the tools you use to access the data (both the input with ETL as well as the output to the user and BI tools). You will only need to make determinations as to which of them will be reusable and which of them will be required to migrate to new and different processes. This book will give you the understanding to help you make informed decisions on these unique things in your environment. On the plus side, if you are already using SQL-based tools for query access or business intelligence tools, technical migration for your end users will be easy. As far as your data warehouse itself is concerned, if your environment is like most well-controlled (or even well thought out) data warehouse implementations, there are always some things that fall into the category of "if I could do that again". Don't leave them on the table now; this is your chance to not only migrate, but to make things better in the process.

In the most general terms, there are no changes necessary for the schema that you are migrating out of and the one that you will build in Redshift to receive the data. As with all generalizations, there are a few caveats to that statement, but most of these will also depend on what database architecture you are migrating from. Some databases define a bit as a Boolean; others define it as a bit itself. In this case, things need to be defined as Boolean. You get the idea; as we delve further into the migration of the data, I will talk about some of the specifics. For now, let's just leave it at the general statement that the database structure you have today can, without large efforts, be converted into the database structures in Redshift. All the kinds of things that you are used to using (private schemas, views, users, objects owned by users, and so on) still apply in the Redshift environment. There are some things, mainly for performance reasons, that have not been implemented in Redshift. As we get further into the implementation and query chapters, I will go into greater detail about these things.

Also, before you can make use of Redshift, there will be things that you will need to think about for security as well. Redshift is run in a hosted environment, so there are a few extra steps to be taken to access the environment as well as the data. I will go through the specifics in the next chapter to get you connected. In general, there are a number of things that Amazon is doing, right from access control, firewalls, and (optionally) encryption of your data, to VPC support. Encryption is one of those options that you need to pick for your cluster when you create it. If you are familiar with Microsoft's **Transparent Data Encryption** (**TDE**), this is essentially the same thing—encryption of your data while it is at rest on the disk. Encryption is also supported in the copy process from the S3 bucket by way of the API interface. So, if you have reason to encrypt your data at rest, Redshift will support it. As you are likely to be aware, encryption does have a CPU cost for encrypting/decrypting data as it is moved to and from the disk. With Redshift, I have not seen a major penalty for using encryption, and I have personally, due to the types of data I need to store, chosen to run with encryption enabled. Amazon has done a thorough job of handling data security in general; however, I still have one bone of contention with the encryption implementation. I am not able to set and manage my own encryption key. Encryption is an option that you select, which then (with a key unknown to me) encrypts the data at rest. I am sure this has to do with the migration of data between nodes and the online resizing operations, but I would still rather manage my own keys. The final part of the security setup is the management of users. In addition to managing the database permissions, as you normally would for users that are accessing your data, there are also cluster-level controls available through Amazon's **Identity and Access Management** (**IAM**) services. These controls will allow you to specify which Amazon accounts have permissions to manage the cluster itself.

When the cluster is created, there is a single database in the cluster. Don't worry; if your environment has some other databases (staging databases, data marts, or others), these databases can be built on the same Redshift cluster if you choose to do so. Within each database, you have the ability to assign permissions to users as you would in the primary database that has been created. Additionally, there are parameter groups that you can define as global settings for all the databases you create in a cluster. So, if you have a particular date format standard, you can set it in the parameter group and it will automatically be applied to all the databases in the cluster.

So, taking a huge leap forward, you have loaded data, you are happy with the number of nodes, and you have tuned things for distribution among the nodes (another topic I will cover later); the most obvious question now to anyone should be: how do I get my data back out? This is where this solution shines over some of the other possible big-data analytical solutions. It really is simple. As the Redshift engine is built on a Postgres foundation, Postgres-compliant ODBC or JDBC drivers will get you there. Beyond the obvious simplicity in connecting with ODBC, there are also a variety of vendors, such as Tableau, Jaspersoft, MicroStrategy, and others, that are partnering with Amazon to optimize their platforms to work with Redshift specifically. There will be no shortage of quality reporting and business intelligence tools that will be available, some of which you likely already have in-house. You can continue to host these internally or on an Amazon EC2 instance. Others will be available as add-on services from Amazon. The main point here is that you will have the flexibility in this area to serve your business needs in the way you think is best. There is no single option that you are required to use with the Redshift platform.

I will also take a closer look at the management of the cluster. As with other AWS service offerings provided by Amazon, a web-based management console is also provided. Through this console, you can manage everything from snapshots to cluster resizing and performance monitoring. When I get to the discussion around the management of your cluster, we will take a closer look at each of the functions that are available from this console as well as the underlying tables that you can directly query for your customized reporting and monitoring needs. For those of you interested in management of the cluster through your own applications, there are API calls available that cover a very wide variety of cluster-management functions, including resizing, rebooting, and others, that are also available through the web-based console. If you are the scripting type, there is a command-line interface available with these management options. As a part of managing the cluster, there are also considerations that need to be given to **Workload Management (WLM)**. Amazon has provided a process by which you can create queues for the queries to run in and processes to manage these queues. The default behavior is five concurrent queries. For your initial setup, this should be fine. We will take a more in-depth look at the WLM configuration later in the book.

As a parting thought in this overview, I would like to provide my thoughts on the future direction the industry in general is taking. I think it is far more than just hype the attention cloud computing, big data, and distributed computing are getting. Some of these are not truly new and innovative ideas in the computing world; however, the reality of all our data-driven environments is one that will require more data to make better, faster decisions at a lower cost. As each year goes by, the data in your organization undergoes its own astronomical "redshift" and rapidly expands (this happens in every other organization as well). The fact that the competitive advantage of better understanding your data through the use of business intelligence will require larger, faster computing is a reality that we will all need to understand. Big data, regardless of *your* definition of big, is clearly here to stay, and it will only get bigger, as will the variety of platforms, databases, and storage types. As with any decision related to how you serve your internal and external data clients, you will need to decide which platform and which storage methodology will suit their needs best. I can say with absolute confidence that there is no single answer to this problem. Redshift, although powerful, is just another tool in your toolbox, and it is not the only answer to your data storage needs. I am certain that if you have spent any amount of time reading about cloud-based storage solutions, you'll surely have come across the term *polyglot*. This term is almost overused at this point; however, the reality is that there are many languages (and by extension, databases and storage methodologies). You will likely not find a single database technology that will fulfill all of your storage and query needs. Understanding this will bring you much closer to embracing your own polyglot environment and using each technology for what it does best.

Summary

In this chapter, we have already covered quite a bit of ground together. From the history of the Redshift implementation to its astronomical roots, you should have a good idea of what your plan is for your initial node configuration and what your choices for encryption are when you allocate a cluster. You should be able to explain to someone why a column store is different from a standard RDBMS storage model. There are many more details for a number of topics that we have touched upon in this overview; however, at this point you should feel like you are not only ready to create your cluster, but to also have an intelligent conversation about Redshift and its capabilities. In the next chapter, we will begin to look at some of the specific things you will need to understand and configure to run your first Redshift cluster.

2

Transition to Redshift

In this chapter, we will build on some of the things you have started thinking about as a result of having read the overview, now that you have made some decisions about which kind of cluster you will be using to start with. We will now get into some of the specifics and details you will need to get up and running. As with most of the Amazon products you have used in the past, there are just a few preliminary things to take care of. You need to have signed up for the Redshift service on the Amazon account you will be using. Although these keys are not specific to Redshift, be sure to hang on to both your public and secret key strings from your user account. Those keys will be labeled `Access Key` and `Secret Key`. You can view the `Access Key` public portion from the user security credentials on the Security Credentials tab. However, if you do not capture the `secret key` when you create the keys, it cannot be recovered and you will need to generate a new key pair. You will need these when we start talking about loading data and configuring the command-line tools. Once you have the permissions for your account, the process to create the cluster is a wizard-driven process that you can launch from your Amazon Redshift management console.

Cluster configurations

You will find that for most things that you deal with on Redshift, the default mode is one of no access (default security group, VPC access, database access, objects in the database, and so on). Due to the fact that you need to deal with that on a consistent basis, you will find that it will not be an issue for you; it will simply be part of the process. Creating objects will require granting permissions as well as granting permissions to access cluster management. Depending on the environment that you are coming from, this may be frustrating sometimes; however, considering the fact that you are remotely hosting your data, I for one am happy with the extra steps necessary to access things. The importance of data security, as a general statement, cannot be overstated. You are responsible for your company's data as well as its image and reputation. Hardly a week goes by without news of companies that have had to make public announcements of data being improperly accessed. The fact that data has been improperly accessed has little to do with the location of the data (remote or local) if you use Amazon or some other provider, but rather it depends on the rules that have been set up to allow access to the data. Do not take your security group's configuration lightly. Only open access to the things you really need and continue to maintain strict database rules on access. Honestly, this should be something you are already doing (regardless of where your data is physically located); however, if you are not, take this as the opportunity to enforce the necessary security to safeguard your data. You will need to add your IP ranges to allow access from the machine(s) that you will be using to access your cluster. In addition, you should add your EC2 security group that contains the EC2 instances (if there are any) that you will be connecting from, as shown in the next screenshot. Later in this chapter, we will cover installation and configuration of the command-line interface using a connection from an EC2 instance. If you don't have an EC2 instance, don't worry, you can still add it later if you find it necessary. Don't get hung up on that, but if you already have the security group, add it now.

You will also need to have a parameter group. A **parameter group** applies to every database within the cluster, so whatever options you choose, think of them as global settings. If there are things that you would like to adjust in these settings, you need to create your own parameter group (you may not edit the default). The creation of the new group may be done before you create your cluster. You will see where you associate the parameter group to the cluster in the next section. If you don't need to change anything about the default values, feel free to simply use the parameter group that is already created, as shown in the following screenshot:

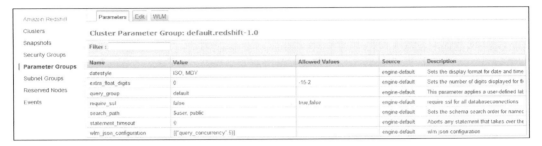

Cluster creation

In this section, we will go through the steps necessary to actually create your cluster. You have already made the "hard" decisions about the kinds of nodes, your initial number of nodes, and whether you are going to use encryption or not. Really, you only have a couple of other things to decide, such as what you want to name your cluster. In addition to the cluster name, you will need to pick your master username and password. Once you have those things decided, you are (quite literally) four simple pages away from having provisioned your first cluster.

 Don't forget, you can resize to a different number of nodes and even a different cluster type later.

Launch the cluster creation wizard by selecting the **Launch Cluster** option from the Amazon Redshift Management console:

This will bring you to the first screen, **CLUSTER DETAILS**, as shown in the following screenshot. Here you will name your cluster, the primary database, your username, and password. As you can see, there are clear onscreen instructions for what is required in each field.

The **NODE CONFIGURATION** screen, shown as follows, will allow you to pick the size of the nodes. You can also select the type of cluster (**Single Node** or **Multi Node**). For this example, I chose **Single Node**.

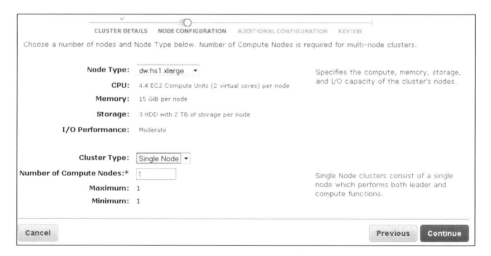

The additional configuration screen, as shown in the next screenshot, is where you will select your parameter group, encryption option, VPC if you choose, as well as the availability zone. A **Virtual Private Cloud (VPC)** is a networking configuration that will enable isolation of your network within the public portion of the cloud. Amazon allows you to manage your own IP ranges. A **Virtual Private Network (VPN)** connection to your VPC is used to essentially extend your own internal network to the resources you have allocated in the cloud. How to set up your VPC goes beyond Redshift as a topic; however, do understand that Redshift will run inside your VPC if you so choose.

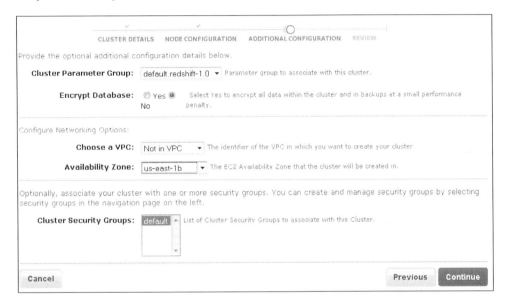

Believe it or not, that really is everything. On the **REVIEW** screen, as shown in the next screenshot, you can now confirm your selections and actually start the cluster. Once you select the **Launch Cluster** button here, it will take a few minutes for your cluster to initialize. Once initialization is complete, your cluster is ready for you to use.

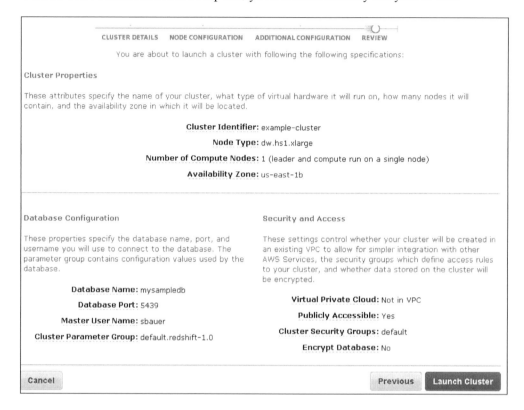

Cluster details

We will take a look at some of the options you have to manage the cluster you have just created in ways other than using the Redshift Management console; however, since we just used the console to create the cluster, we will continue on with that tool for now.

Before we go much further into the details, take a quick look around at the Redshift Management console. You will be quickly comfortable with the options you have available to manage and run your cluster. We will take a much more specific look in a later chapter at the query and performance monitoring parts, as well as the mechanics of restoring and saving snapshots. For now, what you will be interested in are some of the basic status and configuration screens. Once you have your cluster running, the following initial screen giving you the "at a glance" health status is displayed:

Along the left-hand side of the screen, as shown in the following screenshot, you can see some of the high-level management functions related to backups, security groups, and so on.

Once you have selected your cluster, there are some tabs across the top. For now, you can familiarize yourself with these, particularly the **Configuration** screen that you can access from the tab shown in the next screenshot. There is a wealth of information there. Most important (for now), because surely you want to get connected, is the endpoint information.

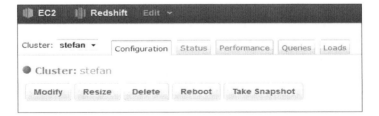

 From the main AWS console, you can drag any of the AWS services you wish up into your own menu bar (see the **EC2** and **Redshift** icons in the preceding screenshot), making it easy to get to the different console views.

Before we go too far and you jump the gun and start connecting tools and loading data, there are a few things to be aware of. I will go into greater detail on the configuration, layout, table creation, and so on as we go further along; so, let's just start with a few high-level things to keep in mind. Although you will be using PostgreSQL drivers, the core of the database is Postgres. There are certain things that have, for performance reasons, been removed. We will shortly take a closer look at the kinds of things that have not been implemented. So, as you mentally prepare the choices for the first tables you will be loading to test with, depending on what environment you are coming from, partitioning, subpartitioning, and range partitioning are the things you will leave on the table. I will explain the concept of distribution keys, which is similar to partitioning but not altogether the same. As a database professional, there are some other core features that you are used to maintaining, thinking about, and optimizing, such as indexing, clustering of data, primary keys, as well as unique constraints on columns. In the traditional sense, none of the clustering options are supported, nor are indexes. I will discuss sort keys and the considerations around what it means to select sort keys later. As far as primary key assignment is concerned, you can, and (depending on the table) maybe should, assign the primary key; however, it does nothing to enforce uniqueness on the table. It will simply be used by the optimizer to make informed decisions as to how to access the data. It tells the optimizer what you, as the user, expect to be unique. If you are not familiar with data warehouse design, you might be thinking "Oh my gosh, what were they thinking?". Those of you familiar with warehouse implementations of large tables are probably already running without primary keys on your largest tables. Load processes are designed to look up keys in dimensions, manage those keys based on the business values, and so on. I am not going to go too far off the topic on dimensional modeling here; that is not really what we are trying to learn. It should be sufficient to say that when you are loading the fact table, by the time you hit the `insert` statement into the fact table, you should have fully-populated dimension keys. Null values would be handled and all of the heavy lifting would be done by the load process. Logically, the overhead incurred by the database's revalidation of all of the things that you just assigned in the load is a very expensive operation when you are dealing with a 100-million row table (Redshift is about eliminating I/O). The same logic applies to the constraints at the column level. You can set the `not null` constraints but do nothing to actually ensure the data matches that expectation. There are a couple of maintenance commands (similar to a statistics update you are likely to be familiar with) after you manipulate large quantities of data that are more important to the optimization process than the application of constraints on the columns. I will get into the details about those commands after we get some data loaded.

SQL Workbench and other query tools

Since you are able to connect to the database with native or ODBC PostgreSQL drivers, your choice of query tools is really and exactly that, *your choice*. It is recommended that you use the PostgreSQL 8.x JDBC and ODBC drivers. Amazon makes a recommendation for a SQL Workbench tool, which for the (free) price will certainly work, having come from environments that have more fully-featured query tools. I was a little frustrated by that product. It left me wanting for more functionalities than is provided in that product. I tried out a few others and finally settled on the SQL Manager Lite tool from the EMS software (a Windows product). Links to this product and other tools are listed in the *Appendix, Reference Materials*. I know it sounds counterintuitive to the discussion we just had about all the features that are not needed or are not supported; so, there are clearly going to be some things in the query tool that you simply will never use. You are after all not managing a traditional PostgreSQL database. However, the ability to have multiple connections, script objects, doc windows, to run explain plans, and to manage the results with the "pivot" type functionality is a great benefit. So, now that I have talked you out of the SQL Workbench tool and into the EMS tool, go and download that. Just to limit the confusion and to translate between tools, the screenshots, descriptions, and query examples from this point forward in this book will be using the EMS tool. Once you have the SQL tool of your choice installed, you will need some connection information from your configuration screen, as shown in the next screenshot. There is a unique endpoint name and a port number. You will also need the master user ID and password. This is your `sysadmin` account that we will be using to create other users, schemas, and so on.

Now that you have everything you need, select the option to create a database connection, plug in the info, and you are now connected to your cluster. If this is really your first remote database, it may be a bit early to declare total victory; however, you have now joined the ranks of the companies that talk about their cloud computing capabilities! I will go into greater detail about schemas and permissions when we discuss the management of your data.

Before we get into loading your data, we will talk about accessing your data with third-party products. There are a variety of ETL tools, and depending on which product you are currently using, you may simply be able to continue with the product you are using. Additionally, there have been some recent partnership announcements from Informatica about providing an Amazon service-based option to use their **PowerCenter** product. If your native expertise is in SSIS, it is possible to connect using ODBC database connections; however, you will have performance issues with large quantities of data without using some data copy options from files. There are other options, such as **Pentaho**, that also have a tremendous amount of promise as well.

As you start to think about your transition to this new environment, you will have a variety of decisions to make that will be unique to the current location of your source data and the in-house expertise that you have for ETL products. The good news is that most of the types of processes you currently support will translate well to Amazon Redshift. There are certain functions in SQL that are not supported; however, for the most part, the insert, update, and delete functionality, right down to creating temp tables in your queries are supported and will translate without major changes. As we get into the next chapter and begin exploring the options you have to load your data, I am confident that you will quickly be up and running with a proof of concept of your own.

Unsupported features

There are a few things to keep in mind that you might be accustomed to using that are different than you might expect or that are simply not available to you. I am not really going back on the statement that there is little change to your SQL. You will find that the majority of your queries will work with little or no modification. This section will highlight what I think will be most important to you as you review the kinds of reporting and analytical processes you have running in your current environment. In addition to the changes in Postgres' functionality, there are a series of Redshift-specific system tables that augment, and in some cases, replace the functionality found in the Postgres system tables. We will look at the system tables specifically as we discuss management and querying later in the book. Just understand that if you are familiar with Postgres' system tables, there are going to be some things that you will need to be aware of.

- **Create table**: This is a standard SQL statement that will allow you to build objects in the database.
  - ○ Tablespaces: These are not supported.
  - ○ Table partitioning: This is not supported; however, there is the distribution key, which is different from traditional partitioning.
  - ○ Inheritance: This is not supported.
  - ○ Unique constraint: This constraint can be created; however, it is used only to inform the optimizer when creating the query plan to access the data. We will review these constraints later as we discuss loading data.
  - ○ Exclusion constraint: This is not supported.
  - ○ Foreign Key: This is informational to the optimizer only.
  - ○ Primary Key: This is informational to the optimizer only.

- **Alter table**: This is a standard SQL statement that will allow you to change the structure of tables.
  - ○ ALTER COLUMN: This is not supported.

- **Copy**: This feature is highly optimized for load purposes and will connect to an Amazon S3 bucket or an Amazon DynamoDB database.

- **Order by**: This standard SQL keyword will affect the order in which the data is output by a query.
  - ○ Nulls: (order by nulls) is not supported.
  - ○ First/Last: (order by first/last) is not supported.

- **VACUUM**: If you are familiar with the Postgres VACUUM function to reorganize tables, this is similar, but with new options to support the Redshift functionality.

- **Insert/Update/Delete**: No worries, these are supported! However, the WITH syntax is not supported.

- **Indexes**: You will find this as one of the management (particularly space management) items that you will not miss. My only concern early on, which as of yet has not been a problem, is the ability to affect a particularly poorly performing query with the help of a well-placed index. This will remain on my "watch list" of things to look out for, but as I said, so far it has not posed any problems.

- **Collations**: Locale-specific or user-defined collation sequences are not supported.

- **Array and Row constructor value expressions**: These are not supported.
- **User-defined functions**: This seems to be a limitation that at some point will need to be addressed. I don't see a technical reason why this was eliminated (but then again, I am not one of the engineers that built Redshift).
- **Stored procedures**: Why this was eliminated is also not clear to me. Building stored procedures, thus incorporating complicated logic into a centralized stored process, seems like it would be something that an analytical database would be able to do.
- **Triggers**: These are not supported.
- **Table functions**: These are not supported and are one of those items based on the column store functionality that may not prove to be necessary. Keep this item in mind as you review your queries for what will be impacted as you move to Redshift.
- **Sequences**: These are not supported.
- **Full text search**: This is not supported.

Without getting too bogged down with the specifics, there are certain SQL related datatypes that are supported on the leader node, where that part of the query will not be passed to the data nodes. There are also datatypes that fall into the category of "unsupported features" that we are discussing here. Some of the unsupported datatypes are slightly more obscure datatypes, such as object identifier types and network address types. Those and a few others, for the sake of clarity, I am leaving off this list. For our purposes here, we will review those datatypes that are simply not available. No caveats here, so you do need to review your SQL. For these, the `create table` statements are not available to you in Redshift.

- **Arrays**
- **Bit/Bit Varying** (ok, so there is a caveat, Boolean works fine)
- **Bytea** (Postgres' binary datatype)
- **Composite types**
- **Date/Time types**:
    - Interval
    - Time
    - Timestamp with timezone
    - Timezone_hour
- **Enumerated types**
- **Geometric types**

- **JSON**
- **XML**
- **Numeric types**:
  - Serial, Bigserial, Smallserial
  - Money (careful here! You will likely have something somewhere in your database defined as money)

Now that we have looked at some of the things that are different as well as the unsupported datatypes that you need to look at in your tables and SQL, there is just one remaining section of unsupported features and those are functions. Similar to the other parts of this section, this is not a complete listing. There are quite a number of these unsupported functions. Please don't be discouraged at this point. Most of these are not likely to impact much of your SQL, particularly standard end user queries. I am simply trying to paint an accurate picture of the things you need to consider.

- **Access privilege inquiry functions**
- **Aggregate functions**: Don't worry; since this could be a hot-button issue for some, I have listed all of them here. As you will see in the following list, I am sure you will find that most of the queries that you have already written do not use these functions:
  - `string_agg()`
  - `array_agg()`
  - `every()`
  - `xml_agg()`
  - `corr()`
  - `covar_pop()`
  - `covar_samp()`
  - `regr_avgx()`
  - `regr_avgy()`
  - `regr_count()`
  - `regr_intercept()`
  - `regr_r2()`
  - `regr_slope()`
  - `regr_sxx()`
  - `regr_sxy()`
  - `regr_syy()`
  - `variance()`

- **Database management functions**:
    - ○ Backup/Restore (these are handled by Redshift snapshots)
    - ○ Database object location functions
    - ○ Database object size functions
- **Date/Time functions**: These are mostly related to the lack of timestamp support that we have already discussed:
    - ○ `clock_timestamp()`
    - ○ `justify_days()/hours()/interval()`
    - ○ `transaction_timestamp()`
    - ○ `to_timestamp()`
- **Greatest()**
- **Least()**
- **JSON functions** (as the JSON datatype is not supported)
- **XML functions** (as the XML datatype is not supported)
- **Mathematical functions**:
    - ○ `div()`
    - ○ `setseed()`
- **Range functions and operators**
- **Sequence manipulation functions**
- **String functions:** There are really only a couple of string functions that you will likely come across with any kind of regularity. Please note that `convert()` and `substr()` are on the list of unsupported functions:
    - ○ `bit_length()`
    - ○ `overlay()`
    - ○ `convert()`
    - ○ `convert_from()`
    - ○ `convert_to()`
    - ○ `encode()`
    - ○ `format()`
    - ○ `quote_nullable()`
    - ○ `regexp_matches()`
    - ○ `regexp_replace()`

- ○ regexp_split_to_array()
- ○ regexp_split_to_table()
- ○ split_part()
- ○ substr()
- ○ translate()

- **Trigger functions** (as triggers themselves are not supported)
- **Window functions** (depending on the types of queries you currently have, the following may be found in your SQL):
  - ○ row_number()
  - ○ percent_rank()
  - ○ cume_dist()

- **Text search functions** (as text search is not supported)
- **System Catalog Functions**: As I have already mentioned, we will cover the use of system tables shortly.

I have tried to give you a sense of the kinds of things that are different. Review the complete listings in the Amazon documentation before you formulate a migration plan for your environment.

Command line

There are a variety of cluster management options that are available to you in addition to the online Redshift Management console. Something many of you will be very quickly comfortable with is the command line. The **command-line interface (CLI)** is currently a developer preview product as a GitHub project. Just as with the other options, I am not going to try to replace the available Amazon documentation here. This is just to serve as a highlight of the steps needed to get you going and to show you some of the kinds of things you can do with the help of some basic examples. The Amazon command line utilizes Python (2.6 or greater) and will run on any operating system that supports Python. If you need assistance with Python, there are many great resources at www.python.org. To install the command-line interface, detailed instructions can be found at http://aws.amazon.com/cli. I will describe the basic steps if you are installing on an existing Amazon EC2 instance. First of all, if you are running on an Amazon EC2 instance, you already have Python installed. To get the command-line packages, run the installation with the following command from an account that has permissions to install software on the server:

```
easy_install awscli
```

Next, you will need to create a file with your Amazon credentials on the EC2 server. Make this file read-only to the user that is executing the commands, as it will contain your private and public Amazon keys. For this example, I called the file `cliconfig.txt`; however, you may call it anything you wish. `[default]` is for the profile. If you use `[default]`, you do not need to specify the profile on the command line. This will allow you different configurations within the same file and you can then specify which profile you wish to use. Keep it simple for now and just use `[default]`.

```
[default]
aws_access_key_id = <Your Access Key>
aws_secret_access_key = <Your Secret Key>
region = us-east-1
```

As we noted earlier when we looked at security, you will need your own credentials to be able to fill in the necessary parts here, and you will also need to pick the region that you have your cluster running in. Once you have that file, export the environmental variable necessary for the command line to understand where the configuration file is (add this to your profile as well, so the next time you connect to the host, this will be set for you already).

```
export AWS_CONFIG_FILE=/home/user/cliconfig.txt
```

Once you have the command-line interface installed, your configuration file created, and the environmental variable set, the following command will confirm whether the command line has been properly installed:

```
asw help
```

To verify that you have everything working for your cluster's connectivity, run the following command:

```
aws redshift help
```

Now that you have the technical parts of the command-line interface working, the basic syntax of the command line for Redshift is as follows:

```
aws redshift operation
```

The following are optional arguments:

```
--output output_format
--region region_name
--debug yes
--profile profile_name
--endpoint-url endpoint_url
```

Note that the default output type is JSON. You can also specify text or CSV.

```
aws redshift describe-cluster
```

Again, this is not intended as a replacement for the available documentation. There are currently over 30 command line operations, each with extensive documentation. Clearly, each of these commands will have a unique set of options that are both required and optional. For our purposes here, I just want you to get a feel of the kinds of things that are possible.

- `create-cluster`
- `delete-cluster`
- `modify-cluster`
- `describe-clusters`
- `reboot-cluster`
- `create-cluster-snapshot`
- `delete-cluster-snapshot`
- `describe-cluster-snapshot`
- `restore-from-cluster-snapshot`
- `describe-resize`

As you can see in the preceding list, the `create-cluster` option will allow you to execute the creation of the cluster from the command line. This would produce the exact same result as having gone through the **Launch Cluster** button from the Redshift Management console that we looked at in the beginning of this chapter. The output from `describe-clusters` of a single-node `xlarge` cluster from the previous command is shown in the following screenshot:

```
"Clusters": [
    {
        "NodeType": "dw.hs1.xlarge",
        "Endpoint": {
            "Port": 5439,
            "Address": "stefan.xxxxxxxxx.xxxxast-1.redshift.amazonaws.com"
        },
        "ClusterVersion": "1.0",
        "PubliclyAccessible": false,
        "PreferredMaintenanceWindow": "tue:03:30-tue:04:00",
        "MasterUsername": "sbauer",
        "Encrypted": true,
        "ClusterParameterGroups": [
            {
                "ParameterApplyStatus": "in-sync",
                "ParameterGroupName": "default.redshift-1.0"
            }
        ],
        "ClusterSecurityGroups": [],
        "AllowVersionUpgrade": true,
        "VpcSecurityGroups": [],
        "VpcId": "xxxxxxxxxxxxxxx",
        "ClusterCreateTime": "2013-03-07T18:27:26.264Z",
        "ClusterSubnetGroupName": "stefantesting",
        "AvailabilityZone": "us-east-1b",
        "AutomatedSnapshotRetentionPeriod": 1,
        "ClusterStatus": "available",
        "ClusterIdentifier": "stefan",
        "DBName": "xxxxxxxxxxx",
        "NumberOfNodes": 1,
        "PendingModifiedValues": {}
    }
],
"ResponseMetadata": {
    "RequestId": "2948b869-90b8-11e2-a5eb-df91b312a53a"
}
```

The same output can be produced as text by adding the -output text to the command line. I am confident that if you have a Unix-scripting background, you will be up and running very quickly with the functionality you find in the command-line interface.

The PSQL command line

If you are interested in running commands other than those available in the CLI interface, you can install the standard Postgres **PSQL** command-line tools. The Amazon CLI tool is clearly focused on management functionality and not on the execution of queries. To connect using the psql command line, you need three values: -h (hostname), -p (port), and -U (user). You will then be prompted for the password as shown in the following command:

```
# psql -h <Endpoint> -p 5439 -U <user>
```

There are many other options to pass in files, how you wish to have the output formatted, or setting variables as described here.

Connection options

The following are the connection options:

- -h, --host=HOSTNAME: This is the database server host or socket directory (default is local socket)
- -p, --port=PORT: This is the database server port (default is 5432)
- -U, --username=USERNAME: This is the database username (default is root)
- -w, --no-password: This never prompts for a password
- -W, --password: This forces a password prompt (this should happen automatically)

Output format options

The following are the output format options:

- -A, --no-align: Denotes the unaligned table output mode
- -F, --field-separator=STRING: Sets the field separator (default is |)
- -H, --html: Denotes the HTML table output mode
- -P, --pset=VAR[=ARG]: Sets the printing option VAR to ARG (see the \pset command)
- -R, --record-separator=STRING: Sets the record separator (default is newline)

- `-t, --tuples-only`: Prints only rows
- `-T, --table-attr=TEXT`: Sets the HTML `table` tag attributes (for example `width` and `border`)
- `-x, --expanded`: Turns on the expanded table's output

General options

The following are general options:

- `-c, --command=COMMAND`: Runs only a single command (SQL or internal) and exits
- `-d, --dbname=DBNAME`: Denotes the database name to connect to (default is `root`)
- `-f, --file=FILENAME`: Executes the commands from a file and then exits
- `-l, --list`: Lists the available databases and then exits
- `-v, --set=, --variable=NAME=VALUE`: Sets the `psql` variable `NAME` to `VALUE`
- `-X, --no-psqlrc`: Prevents the startup file from being read
- `-1, --single-transaction`: Executes the command file as a single transaction

API

Along the same lines as the command-line interface, there is a rich list of over 70 API calls. Just like the command line options, the API functions have a well-defined section in the Amazon documentation. As I noted with the command line, you can see that the same ability to create a cluster exists within the API functions as well as the other cluster management tools you would expect to find.

- `CreateCluster`
- `ModifyCluster`
- `DescribeClusters`
- `DeleteCluster`
- `RebootCluster`
- `DescribeClusterParameters`
- `DescribeClusterSecurityGroups`
- `DescribeEvents`
- `DescribeResize`
- `Snapshot`
- `RestoreClusterFromSnapshot`

The thing to understand at this point is one of flexibility. You have choices on how to connect to the cluster as well as what kinds of tools you wish to use to manage that cluster.

Summary

This chapter has started to bring together the things you will need to consider as you bring your data and processes to the Redshift environment. We have looked at quite a few things to get the cluster running, getting your query tools installed and connected, and even started to understand some of the management functions that you will be using on a daily basis. By this point, you should feel comfortable navigating through the Redshift Management console, have your own cluster running, and have a general understanding of the overall Redshift capabilities. You should also understand some of the limitations that you will need to consider as you begin thinking more closely about your own environment. You are by no means ready to run your production reporting yet; however, you really are closer than you might think. In the next chapter, we will bring together some of the things we have covered in getting your environment configured and we will get your data loaded.

3

Loading Your Data to Redshift

This is where the fun starts, particularly for all of the data warehouse professionals who are reading this book. We will work out some of the details around database permissions, and most importantly, get some data loaded.

Before we get to the data loading part that I just promised you, there are a couple of other high-level things we need to think about. As with some of the other topics we have covered so far, I will go into greater detail later. I feel that if you're starting the thought process about these topics as you learn how to load your data, you will ultimately make decisions on how you set up your database. There are some best practices, in the general data warehousing sense, that are all supported here, such as private schemas, public views, and so on. Personally, I have always been an advocate of a schema that is specific to the warehouse data, and a public set of views that enable access to the data. This allows for table alterations, schema changes, and other maintenance processes simply by controlling which table is accessed by the public view, insulating the user queries entirely from those processes. There have also been several instances where the presentation of the data, either by way of functions, case statements, or otherwise, can simply be altered by a change to the view. The use of views in many cases has insulated the load processes from changes needed to support end user reporting, allowing those processes to be altered and maintained later as necessary. As we get into this chapter, I will assume a certain level of competency in creating files out of your own environment. This is where your understanding of the schema you intend to build and your unique knowledge of your data will become important. Additionally, what you consider to be a "normal" query behavior will become important as we start to think about table design and selection of sort keys and distribution keys. The good news is, once you have some data files to work with, you can easily try a few different distribution key definitions to prove and disprove to yourself how your data is going to perform.

From your current environment, script out a basic fact table and a simple dimension table to join to. Don't worry, you will need to load everything at some point. In order to get some gratification of seeing your familiar queries, with your familiar data running, quickly start with something simple. If you are unable to use your own tables and data, you can download sample files from the U.S. Census database that I will be using as samples from `http://quickfacts.census.gov/qfd/ download_data.html`. These are good (freely available) data sources to illustrate the load processes, as well as to build some queries against. I will be using the `DataSet. txt` and `FIPS_CountyName.txt` data files in this chapter. As I have said previously, I recommend using your own table structures and data, if possible, as you will more quickly be able to realize the benefits of the proof of concept, and besides, seeing your familiar data in queries will give you a great sense of actual runtimes. I found there were a few minor changes to the scripted tables that I needed to make coming out of my environment. Depending on what database engine you are running and what tools you are using to script the `create table` statements, there may be a few other changes you need to apply before you can execute the SQL. For me, I had to convert bit to Boolean and remove the square brackets. Other than that, there was nothing for my basic table structures that I had to change. There is no reason you should not feel right at home at this point with normal `create table as...` syntax. From your perspective, if the database is physically present on the desktop that you are working on, on a server down the hall in the server room, or running on Amazon somewhere else in the world, your connect strings may be different; but once you are connected, there is no real difference to how you run things.

Downloading the example code

You can download the example code files for all Packt books you have purchased from your account at `http://www.packtpub.com`. If you purchased this book elsewhere, you can visit `http://www.packtpub. com/support` and register to have the files e-mailed directly to you

Datatypes

In the previous chapter, we spent some time looking at datatypes that are not supported. Now that we are getting ready to build your first table, let us take a quick look at what datatypes are supported. As I have said previously, there will be very little that you cannot support as you build your tables. The following screenshot shows the datatypes that are supported by Redshift:

Data type	Aliases	Description
SMALLINT	INT2	Signed two-byte integer
INTEGER	INT, INT4	Signed four-byte integer
BIGINT	INT8	Signed eight-byte integer
DECIMAL	NUMERIC	Exact numeric of selectable precision
REAL	FLOAT4	Single precision floating-point number
DOUBLE PRECISION	FLOAT8	Double precision floating-point number
BOOLEAN	BOOL	Logical Boolean (true/false)
CHAR	CHARACTER	Fixed-length character string
VARCHAR	CHARACTER VARYING	Variable-length character string with a user-defined limit
DATE		Calendar date (year, month, day)
TIMESTAMP		Date and time (without time zone)

This next screenshot shows the storage requirements and allowable ranges used by the integer datatypes:

Name	Storage	Range
SMALLINT or INT2	2 bytes	-32768 to +32767
INTEGER, INT, or INT4	4 bytes	-2147483648 to +2147483647
BIGINT or INT8	8 bytes	-9223372036854775807 to 9223372036854775807

The following screenshot shows data storage and precision for decimal datatypes. We will look at compression and how this affects your overall storage in a later chapter.

Name	Storage	Range
REAL or FLOAT4	4 bytes	6 significant digits of precision
DOUBLE PRECISION, FLOAT8, or FLOAT	8 bytes	15 significant digits of precision

Schemas

For this proof of concept, we are going to keep the implementation simple and not worry about schemas and views yet. Clearly, when you are ready to work out your production database schema, you will need to give some thought to those details. This point also brings me to an "early adoption issues" story. Don't worry, this story has a happy ending too. However, this little trick lead to me losing my data and learning about cluster restores early in my testing. My initial configuration, to get things up and running for a proof of concept at the lowest cost, was a single node extra-large cluster. As I saw schemas were supported, I thought, why not go through the handful of extra steps to create the schema and build my target configuration. So, after loading, testing, and making sure I had things the way I wanted them, I resized my cluster to a larger number of nodes to do some performance testing, which is where the story part of this comes in. The resize, because I used private schemas, apparently decided to preserve my schema when my cluster came up in the new configuration, not the data. Now, being a "data guy" this seems like one of those things that any database should do well, as losing data is not a good thing. The silver lining in all of this, through that experience as well as a couple of other minor things that I have run into in my testing, is that I have actually gotten to know some of the fine engineers and project management staff at Amazon, and as I have said before, they have been fantastic in supporting me through these issues. My recovery in the end was simply the restore of my cluster back to the prior single-node snapshot, and I was right back to where I was before the resize. It is through this experience and the absolutely stellar response from the Amazon team that I learned a few lessons about resizing and restoring. In the end, those lessons were valuable for me and and helped Amazon identify some issues, which were quickly addressed and resolved. But now back to the subject at hand—schemas. It is really not as a result of this experience that I am suggesting to use the public schema, because those are issues that are in the rear-view mirror and were immediately patched by Amazon. Getting something running with the least number of steps is really simple. If you choose to use a private schema, there are a few things to consider. Let's take a brief look at those here. The syntax to create the schema is as follows:

```
CREATE SCHEMA schema_name [ AUTHORIZATION username ] [ schema_
element(s) ]
```

The name of the schema is `schema_name`, with `username` being the owner of the schema, and `schema_elements` are the objects you wish to associate with the schema at the time of creation.

> This is not the best name you will ever come across for a schema, but to illustrate the point, use `create schema dw_schema`.

If you choose the schema approach, you will also need to grant permissions to your users to be able to select from that schema. I would suggest, rather than assigning individual user permissions, you should associate your users to a group and then grant the necessary permissions to the group. Individual user permissions get messy, quickly.

```
CREATE GROUP group_name
[ [ WITH ] [ USER username (s)]]
```

The syntax `CREATE GROUP reporting_users` will create a group called `reporting_users`. You can use the `WITH USER` syntax to associate users to the group at the time you create the group. You may then assign permissions at the group level, which will allow users to come and go from the group and not need additional permission management. Don't create so many groups that you lose track of what each is for; however, as a general rule, do not assign permissions at the individual user level.

To grant select on `dw_schema` to the `reporting_users`, group that contains all of your read-only reporting users use the following statement:

```
grant usage on dw_schema to reporting_users;
```

There is also a system parameter, `search_path`, that will control the order in which schemas are searched for an object. If identical objects are found in multiple schemas, you can control which one has priority in terms of what order the objects will be searched for. An additional note about schemas is one of default permissions. By default, all users have `CREATE` and `USAGE` privileges on the `PUBLIC` schema. If you wish to prevent users from creating objects in the `PUBLIC` schema, you need to `REVOKE` that permission from the user.

Use the following statement to remove the ability to create objects in the `PUBLIC` schema:

```
revoke create on dw_schema_schema from public;
```

If a user does not have `USAGE` as a permission, they can only access their own objects; so, `USAGE` on the `PUBLIC` schema is probably fine as you will be building your views to access the data in the `PUBLIC` schema. As you can see, there is nothing hugely complicated here (or that different from other relational databases), but for the sake of keeping things simple, and not having to spend time debugging permission issues, stick with the `PUBLIC` schema. I suggest managing permissions at the schema level. However, if there are specific users that need to be in the superuser group, they need to be granted the permission to `create user`. Users who have that permission are also superusers.

Table creation

Starting with a dimension that you have selected from your environment (or the following code), make the necessary datatype changes. Take a stab at your sort key. I will go into some of the additional rules to apply when creating sort keys; however, for now, pick a column or two that are most likely to be involved in joins and add them to the sort key. As this is a dimension, it may simply be the key from the dimension, but it can be more than that; think about how you will be joining to the table. Once you have the `create table` syntax the way you want it, execute it. And as simple as that, your first (of many) tables has been built.

```
CREATE TABLE all_fips_codes
    (
        fips              VARCHAR(10),
        state_country_state VARCHAR(80)
    ) sortkey(fips);
```

Fact tables are no different, with the exception of the distribution key. You can define a distribution key on a dimension if you wish; however, generally dimensions are not large enough to warrant a distribution key. Unlike `sortkey` where you can have multiple (up to 400 columns for reasons I cannot fathom) columns to form a compound key, this particular option operates on a single column. You can define the distribution key and the sort key as the same column if you wish. For the moment, think about how you are likely to join the data, and what will be the largest quantity of data that you will be joining together (it could be a customer key or it could be a year). Don't perform a huge amount of analysis at this point. You know your data, so pick something logical. If you are unsure, go with what you currently have in your environment as your primary partitioning column. Go through the same mental "how do I join to this table" exercise that you did for the dimension, and create a sort key that covers those columns. If you do not have your own fact table to work with, you can use the following `create table` statement:

```
CREATE TABLE census_data
    (
        fips                    VARCHAR(10),
        pop_estimate            BIGINT,
        pop_estimate_base       BIGINT,
        pop_estimate_chg        DECIMAL(5, 1),
        pop_total               BIGINT,
        pop_total_u_5           DECIMAL(5, 1),
        pop_total_u_18          DECIMAL(5, 1),
        pop_total_o_65          DECIMAL(5, 1),
        pop_total_female        DECIMAL(5, 1),
        pop_total_white         DECIMAL(5, 1),
        pop_total_black         DECIMAL(5, 1),
```

```
        pop_total_am_indian          DECIMAL(5, 1),
        pop_total_asian              DECIMAL(5, 1),
        pop_total_hawaiian           DECIMAL(5, 1),
        pop_total_multi_race         DECIMAL(5, 1),
        pop_total_hispanic           DECIMAL(5, 1),
        pop_total_non_hispanic       DECIMAL(5, 1),
        pop_total_gt_1_year_res      DECIMAL(5, 1),
        pop_total_foeign_born        DECIMAL(5, 1),
        pop_total_foeign_lang        DECIMAL(5, 1),
        pop_total_edu_high_school    DECIMAL(5, 1),
        pop_total_edu_bachelors      DECIMAL(5, 1),
        total_veteran                BIGINT,
        avg_work_travel_time         DECIMAL(5, 1),
        housing_unit_estimate        BIGINT,
        owner_occupied_houseing      DECIMAL(5, 1),
        owner_occupied_multi_unit    DECIMAL(5, 1),
        median_value_owner_occupied  BIGINT,
        households                   BIGINT,
        avg_household_size           DECIMAL(6, 2),
        per_capita_inc               BIGINT,
        median_inc                   BIGINT,
        total_poverty                DECIMAL(5, 1),
        private_non_farm_tot         BIGINT,
        private_non_farm_emp_tot     BIGINT,
        private_non_farm_pay_chng    DECIMAL(5, 1),
        non_employer_tot             BIGINT,
        firms_tot                    BIGINT,
        firms_black_owned            DECIMAL(5, 1),
        firms_am_indian_owned        DECIMAL(5, 1),
        firms_asian_owned            DECIMAL(5, 1),
        firms_hawiian_owned          DECIMAL(5, 1),
        firms_hispanic_owned         DECIMAL(5, 1),
        firms_women_owned            DECIMAL(5, 1),
        manufactur_tot               BIGINT,
        wholesale_trade              BIGINT,
        retail_sales                 BIGINT,
        retail_sales_per_capita      BIGINT,
        accomodations                BIGINT,
        new_housing_permits          BIGINT,
        land_area_sq_mile            DECIMAL(18, 2),
        pop_per_sq_mile              DECIMAL(18, 1)
    )
distkey( fips),

sortkey(fips);
```

As we look further at objects and monitoring, I will discuss quite a number of system tables. In keeping with the "getting started" nature of this book, I will not turn this entirely into a technical manual of system table queries. Amazon has a wealth of detailed information on each system table and what each column contains. I will mention in each of the sections the relevant tables and the kinds of data you can find there. I hope to expose you to the tables you will need and to provide you with enough contexts to understand what you should be looking for. I am sure, as you start to work and understand the environment better, you will find them to be an invaluable resource. Before we dive into our first system table queries, there are a few table naming conventions to be aware of. STL_ is a Redshift system physical table. STV_ is a Redshift system view or "virtual table". These views contain data from the current state of the cluster, and generally only contain data since the last restart. SVV_ are Redshift system views that will combine some of the STL_ and STV_ tables together for commonly used queries. Some of these tables and views are restricted to the superuser group; however, for the purposes of clarity in this book, I will assume that the person running these kinds of queries and setting up the cluster will have superuser permissions. There are certain queries that you will want to expose through reporting, or otherwise, to your end users. Queries about the health and status of the cluster are an administrative function.

For system tables and views that contain a userid column, in general, you will want to limit your queries of those tables to userid greater than 1 to avoid picking up the information that is generated by the Redshift engine.

To be able to see all the system tables in the EMS SQL Manager object explorer, you will need to set the **Show system object** option in the database registration properties, as you can see in the following screenshot, which is not set by default:

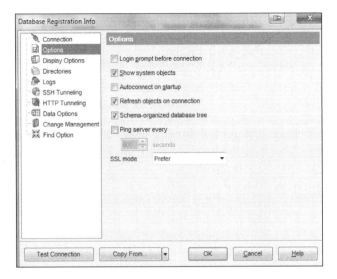

Now that you have run a `create table` statement or two, take a look in the `stl_ddltext` table. In this table, you can see who did what with the following DDL in the database:

```
Select * from stl_ddltext
where userid > 1
order by pid,starttime,sequence
```

Connecting to S3

In the previous chapter, we covered the tools and installed the EMS SQL Manager product that you will need to access the database. As we are now getting ready to load data, you need to have a way to get the data from your local environment into the database. Shortly, I will explain why `insert into` will pose problems. We will be using the `copy` command to move data into the database, which will be reading from S3. As with most things we have discussed to this point with regard to third-party products, you again have options; particularly as you are now going to connect to Amazon S3, which has been around for a while. If you don't want to use the Amazon S3 managing service, the other two solutions that I have found, which are both good and easy-to-use, are the Firefox plugin by `www.s3fox.net` called **S3Fox**, and the desktop software **Cloudberry Explorer** from Cloudberry Lab (`http://www.cloudberrylab.com/free-amazon-s3-explorer-cloudfront-IAM.aspx`). Both solutions will allow you to transfer data from your network or local machine up to your S3 bucket. I chose to use the Cloudberry Explorer desktop software for its ability to upload large files and to support encryption. Do note however that the free version does not support encrypted files, and it has the same 5 GB per file limit that you will have using S3Fox. However, if encryption of data on S3, files greater than 5 GB, retrieval from FTP sites, or scripting are in your future, start with Cloudberry Explorer, as their pro version has some of the features you will need. Don't worry, 5 GB will be fine for now (and in reality, probably even for production size files). Even if you have monster sized files, the copy supports compression in the data load. I would suggest that it is well worth the effort, relative to the time it takes to upload and the minimal cost in CPU time to uncompress at load time, to compress your data before uploading to your S3 bucket. The next screenshot shows how to connect using Cloudberry Explorer. Simply provide a display name you like, your access key, and a secret key.

Beyond the use of compression for your data files, there are some clear advantages to splitting the data files into logical sections of data. They don't need to match your distribution key or anything else that you set up in the database. However, multiple files for a given table will help you load in parallel. Multiple files will also assist you in isolating failures into particular files. We will look at troubleshooting and the system tables involved shortly. As I mentioned previously, when you were creating your tables, having some reasonably sized files to load will also enable you to perform side-by-side comparison on some of the distribution key options by reloading portions of tables into different configurations.

If you are not working with the sample files, and if you have the kind of luck that I do, you will run into characters in your data that will not fit into the target code page. As you look at the kind of data that you are storing, you will find (or at least I did) some characters that need to be removed. You can handle them on export. As you think about your load processes that you need to build, depending on your sources, you will need to account for these situations in the **Extract Transform and Load** (ETL) process that you build. I had exported almost 60 million records into each of several files using a bulk export process out of my current database. Rather than slowing down that entire process and building a custom extract to handle these, I fell back to a process that works very well on files and wrote a quick Perl script (as shown in the following code) to remove the non-ASCII characters. So, while I was reading and re-writing the files, I took the opportunity to split the files into 10 million row chunks. This provided me files that for testing purposes were right at 3 GB per file (which via normal compression levels end up below 500 MB). Perl is available for any operating system; **ActivePerl** (http://www.activestate.com/activeperl) for Windows is fine. You can simply run the installer, and you don't need additional modules or anything else to make this work. The script found in this example takes in a file as an argument, opens an output file with the same name, an incremented number, and splits the file while removing extra carriage returns (015) as well as non-ASCII characters. I am in no way saying that this will be necessary for your data, I am just trying to give you a starting point should you find your back up against a wall and you are looking for a way to get your proof of concept running quickly.

```perl
#!/usr/bin/perl -w

$file=$ARGV[0];

if(!$file) {
  print "$0 <file> \n";
  exit(1);
}


open($fh, "< $file") or die "Unable to open $file";
```

```
$headers=<$fh>;   # Read

$rc=0;
$file_cnt=1;


$file_out = $file . "_" . $file_cnt;

while($line=<$fh>) {
    open($fho, "> $file_out") or die "Unable to open $file_out";


    while ($rc < 10000000) {
    $line=~s/\015//g;
    $line=~s/[^[:ascii:]]//g;
    $rc++;
    print $fho $line;
    $line=<$fh>;

    if (eof($fh))
        {
        close ($fh);
         close ($fho);
        exit(0);
        }
    }
close ($fho);
$rc = 0;


$file_cnt= $file_cnt + 1;
$file_out = $file . "_" . $file_cnt;
}

close ($fh);
close ($fho);

exit(0);
```

I know by now it might feel like you have done a lot of work to get to this point; however, with the exception of the table creation, we have not really spent a lot of time running things directly in the database. That is about to change! Now that you have built data files and you are connected to your S3 bucket, we will copy a few files. You are ready to move on to the part of the chapter that will be most satisfying; copying data into your tables. If you are not working with your own data files, download the `DataSet.txt` and `FIPS_CountyName.txt` data files from `http://quickfacts.census.gov/qfd/download_data.html` if you have not already done so. These files will match the layouts of the tables you built with the `create table` scripts for the `all_fips_codes` dimension as well as the `census_data` fact table. You can (optionally) compress the file with gzip before you copy it to your S3 bucket. For simplicity, and the small size of the file, you can simply copy the file without compressing it first. If you do compress it, you will need to add the `-gzip` option to the `copy` command.

> Before you upload the `DataSet.txt` file to your S3 bucket, remove the header row that contains the column names.

The copy command

Now that you have copied the sample data files to your S3 bucket, we can actually copy the data into the tables. There are two `copy` commands that we will now review, the first one of which will load the dimension. I have used a fixed layout definition for this data file.

```
copy all_fips_codes from 's3://testing/redshift/FIPS_CountyName.txt'
credentials
'aws_access_key_id=<yourkey>;aws_secret_access_key=<yourkey>'
fixedwidth '0:5,1:50';
```

As this is the first `copy` command, let's take it a little slow and walk through the command and the options I have supplied:

- `copy`: The `copy` command
- `all_fips_codes`: This is the target table
- `from 'S3 bucket/FIPS_Countyname.txt'`: This is the S3 bucket location and the file you uploaded

- credentials 'aws_access_key_id; aws_secret_access_key': This is your credentials to connect to Amazon (the same ones you used to connect to the S3 bucket) and the command-line interface in the previous chapter

- fixedwidth 'col:len, col:len...': These can be a column name, or can simply be numbered; 'fips:5, state_country_state:50' would also be valid

The next copy command you issue has a different target table and a different source file. This copy command is showing you how to issue a command for a delimited file:

```
copy census_data from 's3://testing/redshift/DataSet.txt'
credentials
'aws_access_key_id=<yourkey>;aws_secret_access_key=<yourkey>'
delimiter ',';
```

The only difference in options between these two copy commands is the use of delimiter rather than fixedwidth. There are a variety of options to the copy command, as you can see in the following screenshot, dealing with everything from date formatting to null handling and others:

```
COPY table_name [ (column1 [,column2, ...]) ]
FROM 's3://objectpath'
[ WITH ] CREDENTIALS [AS] 'aws_access_credentials'
[ option [ ... ] ]

where option is

{ DELIMITER [ AS ] 'delimiter_char'
  FIXEDWIDTH 'fixedwidth_spec' }
  ENCRYPTED
  GZIP
  REMOVEQUOTES
  EXPLICIT_IDS
  MAXERROR [ AS ] error_count
  DATEFORMAT [ AS ] 'dateformat_string'
  TIMEFORMAT [ AS ] 'timeformat_string'
  IGNOREHEADER [ AS ] number_rows
  ACCEPTANYDATE
  IGNOREBLANKLINES
  TRUNCATECOLUMNS
  FILLRECORD
  TRIMBLANKS
  NOLOAD
  NULL [ AS ] 'null_string'
  EMPTYASNULL
  BLANKSASNULL
  COMPROWS numrows
  COMPUPDATE [ { ON | TRUE} | { OFF | FALSE } ]
  STATUPDATE [ { ON | TRUE} | { OFF | FALSE } ]
  ESCAPE
  ROUNDEC
```

We will now look further into tracking load times and how to manage parallelism with the loads. There is a system table named `stl_s3client` that you can review to track the time spent in data transfer from S3 as part of your copy operation. The copy operation is supported from both S3 as well as Amazon's DynamoDB. Although it looks like you should be able to put a network share or local file location in the `copy` command, it will only work as a server-side operation connecting to S3 files or DynamoDB. If you are copying from DynamoDB tables, keep in mind that you are paying for provisioned throughput (it will cost you to read data out even if you are just pulling it into Redshift). There is an option that you can add to the `copy` command (`readratio xx`) where you can specify the total percent of provisioned throughput you will allow to be used. The options for the DynamoDB `copy` command (in the next screenshot) show the `readratio`, as well as things such as `noload` (test run without copying any data to find out if you have issues before you begin the actual copy):

```
where option is

    EXPLICIT_IDS
    MAXERROR  [ AS ]  error_count
    DATEFORMAT [ AS ]  'dateformat_string'
    TIMEFORMAT [ AS ]  'timeformat_string'
    ACCEPTANYDATE
    TRUNCATECOLUMNS
    TRIMBLANKS
    NOLOAD
    EMPTYASNULL
    BLANKSASNULL
    COMPROWS numrows
    COMPUPDATE  [ {  ON  | TRUE}  | {  OFF  | FALSE  } ]
    STATUPDATE  [ {  ON  | TRUE}  | {  OFF  | FALSE  } ]
    ROUNDEC
```

Load troubleshooting

If you are anything like me and you read the part about splitting files and scrubbing the non-ASCII characters earlier in this chapter, you might say "what the heck, let's try it without all that" (as you probably should have). If you did, you may have already found this table all on your own. However, as with any load process, determining errors and diagnosing the cause is a critically important part of the process, so let's take a little bit of a detour into diagnosing load errors. The following are a few tables that you will be using:

- STL_load_errors: This contains information about the particular error that was encountered during the load. This table will capture the actual column as well as the data that is causing the error.

- STL_loaderror_detail: This contains detailed data for an error that you encountered and found in the STL_load_errors table. This table will provide several rows of good data for the column that caused the error, as well as the column and data that caused the issue. For example, if you had an "invalid digit" error in a column named dt_key, it would provide you the example data of the valid rows preceding the row that had the error; such as 20130115, 20130201 listing out the column dt_key, followed by 1st Street for column dt_key. Using this information, you can see that you have something misaligned in the input data file, or simply bad data in the column for dt_key. You also have enough information to find the offending row and address the root cause of the issue.

- STV_load_state: This contains the current state of the copy commands including the percent complete of the data loads.

- STL_tr_conflict: This contains information about errors involving locking issues. I list this one here as it is a logical issue you can run into during data load; however, this table will be useful for other troubleshooting purposes as well.

- STL_file_scan: This contains information about which files on which nodes were accessed during the data copy operation.

- STL_load_commits: This contains information about which query, which filename, how many rows, and which slice was affected by a load. I hate to throw a new term out and then leave you hanging; however, we will discuss slices when we look at distribution keys at the end of this chapter.

With the use of these system tables, you should be able to identify, diagnose, and repair all of the load errors that you encounter during the copy operation. These load-specific tables will only be populated if you are running the `copy` command loading data from the S3 server share. Amazon has put a large amount of effort into the optimization, error identification, and monitoring of load processes that are running the `copy` command. At this point, I will sidetrack us for a "short story" again, which similar to my other story ends up involving some conversations with Amazon engineers, and also has a happy ending. I again learned some lessons—as I learn most of my life lessons—the hard way.

From a lack of understanding on my part of how data needed to be loaded, my desire to quickly get data into the database, and a desire to avoid unencrypted data files, I chose to try copying data without using the `copy` command. This was my first attempt to load data into Redshift with any kind of large volume of data from files. I built on the filesystem with an `insert into … values...` statement with a large quantity of data attached. I did some scripting to process my pipe-delimited output file from the database and reconstructed it as a comma-delimited `insert` statement. So, the first lesson I learned is that there is a 16 MB limit to the size of a single SQL statement you can pass to the Redshift engine. (I know I had the engineers scratching their heads at this point... whoever imagined someone will pass a 300 MB or larger SQL statement? Yes, that would be me...). Well, that was no deterrent. I figured multiple files would be better for parallel loading anyway, so once the size issue was handled, and the file was broken into small enough pieces, I thought I had this thing working. I had 25,000 row chunks of data loading at a speed of just over 20 seconds per chunk; so who would not go parallel to see how fast it would go and to see at what point things would degrade? You guessed correctly again, that would be me. I also found that the database does not handle that kind of processing well (or gracefully). Multiple crashes of the database later (and a patch, which did dramatically improve things, but not completely resolve the issue) made it clear (ok, to be fair, I was told) that this was not really going to work as any kind of a long-term solution. Not only was my approach not the recommended method, it was not particularly fast, even in parallel. Once I accepted this, I copied my data to S3; even as compressed files, I was getting load speeds into the database well over 100 times faster with the recommended copy methodology. In addition to the fantastic speed improvements, debugging failures, data conversion issues, and monitoring suddenly were transformed from a guessing game to a rather precise process of running queries and checking statuses on the Redshift Management console. So, the moral of my trip down story lane is not necessarily that you should not push the boundaries and try things that are outside the box, just understand when you are outside the box. If you know when you are outside the box, it is also important to know when it is best to accept the recommendation of the developers and engineers to get back in the box.

Primarily for testing purposes, if you are having difficulty with your
data formats, you may consider setting a reasonable error count so
you can get some of your data into the database to work with.
```
MAXERROR [as] error_count
```

Selecting from the error table after an error (which you will actually be directed to do
in the error message), you will find a good bit of information. It actually quite clearly
identifies the error. In the case I have illustrated in the next example, the value in
`raw_field_value` simply will not fit into an `int4` datatype for the `wholesale_trade`
column. You are also given the filename, position within the row, and the `raw_line`
of data so that you can specifically locate the error.

```
select * from stl_load_errors
```

colname	type	raw_field_value	err_reason	filename	position	raw_line
wholesale_trade	int4	4174286516	Overflow (Integer valid range -2147483648 to 2147483647)	redshift/DataSet.txt	270	00000,313914040,308747508,1.7,308745538,6

Earlier, I had also mentioned the `stl_load_error_detail` table. Remember that
table as well if the error is not as simple and obvious as this one.

ETL products

Now that you are moving forward with the `copy` command, you are well on your way to building an environment that can service your analytical needs in a variety of ways. One of the decisions you will need to make is around your choice of ETL product. Much of that will have to do with what kinds of sources you are dealing with, how often you need the data refreshed, what kinds of data volume are you trying to load, as well as a variety of other factors; not the least of which is the skill set of your existing staff. I can tell you from personal experience with some of the better known tools from Informatica and SSIS to Ab Inetio, as well as several smaller, lesser known products, they each have some inherent strengths (and weaknesses). The Gartner group regularly produces the *Magic Quadrant* report for software products, and the big-name players land in about the places you would expect, as shown in the following figure:

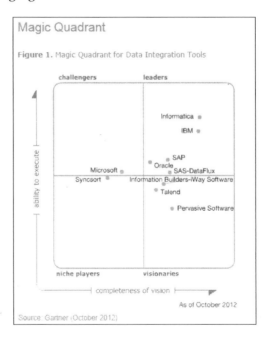

There are others, such as Pentaho and Apatar, that can provide you an open source solution (such as Talend, which is on the Gartner list). Since I seem to be recommending third-party products in groups of two, why stop that now... Of all of the options, I have two clear winners: Informatica and Pentaho. Which of these products you choose will depend largely on your budget and current setup. Informatica has already released their plugin for Redshift to load data using your current Informatica installation. If you have a local installation of Informatica PowerCenter, you can already use your processes to load data to Redshift. Additionally, as an Amazon Redshift partner, Informatica has announced plans to build a PowerCenter version that will run at Amazon as a service. Once this becomes available, Informatica would be a software offering that you can select and configure within your AWS account. It is hard to make a case that Informatica has not been, and will not continue to be, a very strong contender in the ETL space. With Pentaho on the other hand, you can get an enterprise version with support, or you can go with the Kettle open source version. Either way, you get a very capable tool that also includes the reporting functionality and support for a variety of big data sources and targets including Hbase. The reason that I land on Pentaho as the alternative to Informatica is to give you a viable option that has support for the JDBC drivers and a large community of active developers at a significantly reduced cost. My suggestion of these two products does not mean the others will not work; I am simply trying to highlight some options at both ends of the spectrum. In addition to some of the traditional ETL tools, there are also a variety of products from major industry players to start-ups such as Hapyrus that are building interfaces to move data into Redshift in a variety of ways. The thing that is clear to me in seeing the number of partnerships that Amazon already has developed for Redshift, and the number being added, is that the industry has taken notice of Redshift.

Performance monitoring

Now that you have the high-level concept of loading data, there are a few monitoring pages on the Redshift Monitoring console that you will want to take a look at. By selecting the **Performance** tab, you will be presented a series of graphs. I will get to the queries that use the system tables that support these graphs when we look at query monitoring in a later chapter. The following graph takes a look at CPU utilization as well as network throughput. You will see, in a two node configuration, there are actually three lines on the graph; the **Leader**, as well as the two **Compute** nodes. Nothing of what you see here in these two graphs should surprise you. As a data copy load is started, CPU and network resources are used.

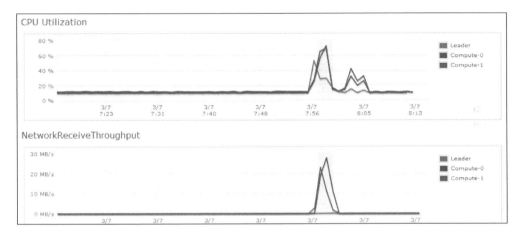

@awscloud @Werner Amazon
#Redshift, it's all about data
compression !

As you look beyond those graphs, you will get to the graphs that all data warehouse professionals should be monitoring on their own systems, and which they should understand in detail to know if their system is performing "normally", or if there are issues that need to be addressed. Those are **Write Latency**, **Read IOPS**, and **Read Throughput**, as shown in the following screenshot. This is where I found things to be impressive (from a metric perspective), without even looking at query run-times. You will also notice that these three graphs are focused solely on the data nodes and do not include any statistics for the leader node. The leader node is exactly that, the leader node for the cluster, and does it not (unless you are running in a single-node configuration) contain any data. A single-node configuration will contain only one line for all of the graphs, as it is a single instance running both leader and data nodes together.

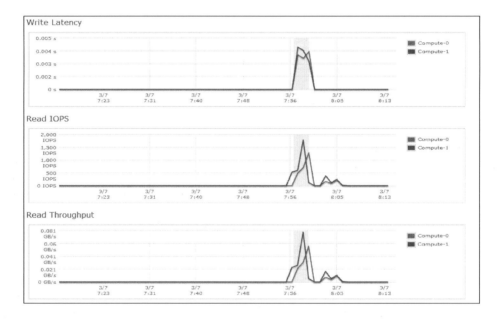

The remaining three graphs found in the following screenshot are directly related to load performance, these are; **Read Latency**, **Swap Usage**, and **Freeable Memory**. As you can see, you should be able to come to this **Performance** tab on the Redshift Management console, and with relative ease, be able to determine the current (and historical) performance of your cluster.

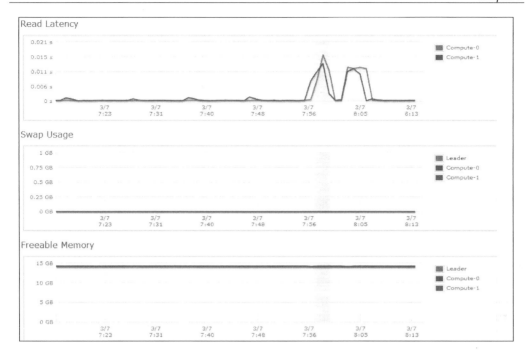

As I have mentioned in passing before, you should not run (other than your testing and setup) on a single node. There are two primary reasons for this, the first being data protection. Data is actually replicated between the nodes. If one of the drives on a node were to fail, that data is resident on another node and will be automatically recovered, which would happen completely transparently to you. The second reason is one of performance. Now, you might argue that I have my order wrong and it should be for performance first. I, however, believe data protection is always at the top of the list. Redshift is designed with the intention of utilizing multiple nodes and running queries in parallel. While you can achieve some parallelism on a single node with multiple processors, the true power really comes from spreading that load across multiple machines. We are talking here about parallel data loading; however, the same principles apply when we look at querying the data across multiple nodes (multiple nodes will always outperform a single node). When we look at resizing as well as running queries, you will see some of the query run-times for the different node configurations.

Indexing strategies

I would imagine that by this time in the book, you would have expected some syntax and discussion of indexing strategies. Well, despite the heading for this section, that is not happening here. As I have mentioned before, there are things that Redshift has done that is different from other conventional relational databases. Based on the fact that the data is stored in a column store as well as the basic premise of eliminating I/O, there simply are no indexes. Now, before I just leave it at that, which really is just about it, you can build (optional) primary keys and (optional) column-level constraints. I call them optional because they are not enforced, and their only purpose is to inform the optimizer to help make better query decisions. Good query optimization decisions are important in any database. Any information you can provide to the optimizer about your data and tables should be provided if you can. So, just because there are no traditional indexes, building a primary key is still a good idea.

Sort keys

Now that we have talked about the lack of indexes, and the fact that there is no need to worry about indexing strategies, I will take part of that back, as you do need to think about how your data will most likely be accessed. The sort key can be between 1 and 400 columns. Before you dump a bunch of things into the sort key, understand that those columns that you put into the sort key are building a compound key, not a set of individual sorts on individual columns. Data, when loaded to your tables, will be sorted based on the column(s) that you have in your sort key. This will have a tremendous effect on your query performance. Think of this as the indexing strategy for Redshift. As columns are joined between tables, if the data is already sorted, the engine can use a merge join, which will be more efficient than a hash join. Just as importantly, as we discussed during our look at how column store data is laid out, the zone mapping that allows entire sections of blocks to be eliminated from the query is developed using the sort key. If the data is sorted and you perform a query that has a filter criteria (for example, `year > 2010`), if your `year` column is sorted, the only blocks that will be read are the ones that contain data with years greater than 2010. Just like indexing strategies in your current environment, there is a little bit of "art" when making decisions about what should go into your sort key. This "art" and your knowledge of your specific data make it difficult for me to generalize; however, to get you started, consider the following:

- A field that is frequently used with the `where` clause to eliminate data, particularly if that data is highly selective, would make a good sort key.
- A datestamp of the data as it is being loaded would make a good sort key.

- A field that is frequently used to join to other tables would make a good sort key, particularly if you are able to make it the sort key for both tables. This will allow the engine to merge join the selected columns very quickly.

- Columns that are used to declare the primary key are generally a good choice for the sort key. Those columns define uniqueness, and will also often be what is joined to, filtered on, and aggregated by.

- If you have data that is used in group by and order by operations on a consistent basis, those are a good choice for the sort key.

Compression will be covered in detail in a later chapter. However, it is important to note that compression encoding should not be applied to columns in your sort key.

Distribution keys

To round out the discussion on things that you need to consider about your data as you build your tables is the distribution key. Redshift will both distribute and replicate data among nodes to achieve the massive parallelism that helps produce such good results. The distribution key is an important part of that process. It is best to try to keep together the largest amounts of data that you will be joining to avoid cross-node joins of large datasets whenever possible. Although these nodes are interconnected on a very high-speed network, the less data that you need to combine across servers in large joins, the better off you will ultimately be. The distribution key will define which data should be kept together on a given node. Unlike the sort key, there is only a single column that can be used in your distribution key. If your source system has a single-column primary key, this is likely a good candidate for the distribution key, as it will provide for even distribution of the data across all of the available nodes. If you do not have (and almost never do in a warehouse fact table) such a key, try to think of something that is at a low enough granularity to provide distribution of data, without having to bring the data back together from different nodes for normal queries. Be careful, however, if you use something like a customer key, as you may only be using a single node to answer a given query. The distribution key is what will be used to divide the data among the nodes and then into slices. A slice is set to the number of cores on a given node, so if the node is a quad-core 2 CPU node, there will be four slices (one for each core) that data is loaded into. Data that is loaded to two nodes will be distributed among eight slices. The more you can do to help the database engine not to have to join those slices across the nodes themselves, the better your query performance will ultimately be. Do not be overly concerned with reading data you don't need. Redshift is optimized for large I/O requests, and ensuring that multiple nodes participate in the query with the distribution key is more important than trying to minimize I/O for a particular query. Distribution of the data across the cluster is really the goal.

Summary

This chapter has increased your understanding of what is most likely the most important part of any data warehouse database—loading data. We covered a lot of ground in this chapter, everything from creating tables to understanding sort keys and the physical mechanics needed to copy data to your cluster. We started to look at what is available for system tables, and even had a discussion on what kind of ETL tools to consider. Don't worry, I am not quite ready to cut you loose on your own. However, after getting your cluster running, building some tables, and loading data, you should feel pretty good about how far you have come in a very short amount of time. The next chapter will go into the details of managing your data, and before you know it, you too will be on your own running a large-scale data warehouse on Redshift.

4
Managing Your Data

This chapter will primarily focus on the management and maintenance functions within Redshift. We have already looked at some of the tools that you have at your disposal to interface with much of this functionality, whether it is from the command-line interface, the API calls, or the Redshift Management console itself. You will gain a good understanding of some of the day-to-day management tasks associated with running a Redshift cluster, including some of the database maintenance functionalities you need to consider.

As a data warehouse administrator, there are many logical as well as physical things that you and your DBA team are used to managing. With Amazon Redshift, you will find that for the most part, the overheads you had in monitoring index health, space, the number of datafiles, and backups have gone away. In addition to these things, the traditional roles that your information technology staff provides for you in SAN management, disk replacement, and general hardware management, have also been taken on by Amazon. Although Amazon has taken on the physical infrastructure tasks, you still have decisions to make. You will still have to manage your data model, make decisions about compression, provide query tuning, as well as general performance monitoring. You also have some new tasks as they relate to VPC management, access management for the Amazon infrastructure, and monitoring of those resources. The physical management of the infrastructure, however, has been taken off your plate. As with many things in life, there are trade-offs. As you no longer have to worry about hardware, operating system patches, database upgrades, and the like, you are giving up some of the control you are used to having. You may or may not have noticed as you made your selections for your cluster that there is a 30-minute window during which Amazon will apply patches and perform other maintenance tasks. Don't worry, you can pick a new time if you did not realize what you were selecting. However, you do need to have a maintenance time for your cluster. You may choose, if you wish, to have database upgrades applied or not; however, the maintenance window itself is not optional. I am not saying that is a bad thing, you just need to be aware that there is a 30-minute window every week where your cluster may not be available. You need to build your processing to accommodate that.

Backup and recovery

Before we get into any of the more interesting topics of this chapter, we need to cover (arguably the least rewarding, but most important) tasks we are responsible for. As the steward of your corporate data warehouse, one key capability is the ability to recover data. This environment is no different, the techniques are just different. Each node that you have running automatically comes with the equivalent amount of backup storage, so there is nothing additional to purchase. Backups are in the form of cluster snapshots. So, if you are accustomed to some of the commercially available backup and recovery tools, such as Redgate, Rman, or otherwise, there are a few things that are important to understand about what a cluster snapshot is:

- Cluster snapshots are a picture of the complete cluster, including the number of nodes. You can neither take a two-node cluster snapshot and do anything other than restore the two-node cluster (even if it would fit into a single node), nor can you take a two-node cluster snapshot and restore it to a three-node cluster. It is a snapshot of the cluster exactly as it is at the point the snapshot is taken.

- There is no way to do table-level recovery. The only option you have to recover data is a complete restore.

- I am sure at some point in your DBA life you have restored a database to a different name to recover a particular table. We will look at what you have available to you for that here as well.

- Clusters are read-only while data is being restored. The cluster is actually available for queries while the restore operation is in progress. Yes, you can also start a restore and run queries at the same time. If you don't already have the data you need to answer the query restored, the restore process will pause your query, wait for the data it needs to be restored, and then resume the query.

- I realize that I have said the same thing a few different ways here, and just to belabor the point one more time, you are taking a snapshot exactly as you would with your camera; a picture frozen in time. It is not incremental, it is not based on logs, and it is not cumulative since the previous image. A database snapshot, just like that photograph, is static—no more data modification is possible to that frame. There is no need to use Photoshop and there is no cropping or editing to get a part of the picture that you like. You may at any point copy that image back in place and go back to that moment in time where you took the picture.

The mechanics of taking backups is simple (it is done for you). Just follow these steps to do so:

1. On the left-hand side of the menu, as the following screenshot shows, (from the Redshift Management console) select **Snapshots**:

2. Once you select the **Snapshots** menu option, you will have several things that you will see, as shown in the following screenshot. Based on the time range in the filter, you can pick which cluster and what time range you wish to review the snapshots for. You can also see snapshot types, which will indicate the automated and manually created snapshots.

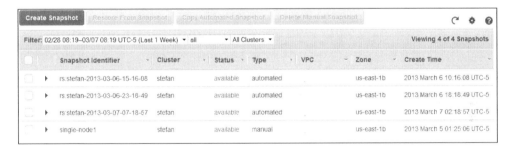

3. If you select one of the snapshots by clicking on the square radio button next to the snapshot, you will be presented with additional information about that snapshot, so you can decide if that is in fact the one you wish to work with for a restore, copy, and so on, as shown in the next screenshot:

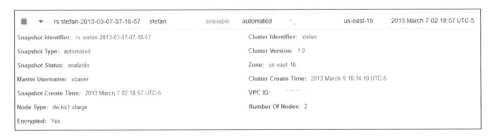

4. It is in this view that you will see the size and quantity of nodes, and also the version of the engine (1.0 in this case) the snapshot applies to. If you wish to create a manual snapshot, it is as easy as selecting the **Create Snapshot** button. Then, give the snapshot an identifier, as shown in the following screenshot (normally something with the date/time is a good idea):

5. A restore of a cluster is no more complicated than the process of creating the snapshot. You find the snapshot you wish to restore by searching/filtering and then selecting the one you wish to use (verify the formation that we saw in the earlier screenshot). Once selected, you select the **Restore Cluster From Snapshot** option. You are then presented with a dialog window, as shown in the next screenshot, which allows you to configure the name and location of where you wish to restore this cluster to. Keep in mind that if you are restoring to a new cluster name, you are starting a second cluster, and will be billed at whatever size/rate is appropriate for this new cluster. By restoring to a new cluster, this is how you can recover a specific table:

6. If you wish to lay the same name cluster back down exactly as it was when the snapshot was taken, you must first delete the cluster, which is an option in the **Clusters** menu. You cannot overwrite a cluster with the same name. No worries, that is exactly how I recovered from the mishap with the resize I discussed in the previous chapter. It worked perfectly with no additional configuration needed. As you see from the screenshots of the different backup operations and information about the clusters, there is nothing really all that complicated here. Being able to query from a cluster while the restoration is happening is a powerful feature, and is one that I hope to never (or at least *very* rarely) need; however, it's good to know it is there. In general, I am one that likes to know that I have tested and proven backup and restore methodologies, and then use them as little as possible!

Resize

One of the key things that cloud computing in general has brought to the industry is the elastic capacity of being able to allocate additional resources as it becomes necessary, and again shrink that capacity when it is no longer needed. There are a couple of points to understand how this works for Redshift. In general, this is a powerful and inexpensive tool to have at your disposal. Depending on your daily workload, for an enterprise data warehouse, you may not have a tremendous need for elastic capacity on a periodic basis. Personally, I work in an environment that will require a much higher (computing) capacity two times a year. With Redshift, you can size up to as many nodes as necessary with no changes to your load processes, query processes, or any other connected tools. There are several things to be aware of with resizing, which are as follows:

- Only the XL (the smaller of the two available configurations) is available in a single node configuration. If you start with the 8XL cluster, the smallest configuration is a two-node one.

- This may be obvious (at least I think it should be) if you have 4.5 TB of data. You cannot size down to a two-node configuration with 4 TB of space without unloading some data to S3, or in some other way reducing the data storage capacity needs.

- You cannot write to the database while a resize operation is in progress.

- The switch to the read-only mode while the resize process is happening will interrupt any running query. From a load perspective, this is likely not a big deal, as you will be resizing as a "planned event". This is not dynamic allocation of resources based on current system demands, although there are API and command-line options for cluster management that allow you to resize. My point here is not the method that starts the resize, but rather that it is not elastic, like dynamically reacting to system loads. Resizing is something you plan for as there is an impact to processes, including those that use temporary tables.

Keeping those points in mind, the resize process itself is straightforward. From the left-hand side of the menu, as shown in the following screenshot, select the **Clusters** option as we had done previously:

From the **Configuration** tab, you can simply select the **Resize** option. You will then fill out the options for the size cluster you wish to move to (up or down, different nodes, and so on). Do keep in mind however that, these sizing changes will have a billing impact.

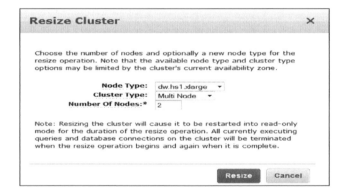

That is all there is to it! There is a reminder note on the screen before you start the resize about the disruptive nature of the resize in regards to running queries, as well as the fact that the cluster will be in read-only while the resize is taking place. Once you start the resize, there is a lag for a few minutes (although the cluster will change the status immediately) before your executing queries will be impacted. During this time, the new configuration is being provisioned. Once that is done and the actual data migration starts, you will automatically switch to the read-only mode for the duration of the operation. In the **Cluster Status** screen, you will be notified that the resize is currently in process, as shown in the following screenshot:

In addition to the status on the **Configuration** tab, the **Status** tab, which is shown in the next screenshot, will also indicate that the resizing is taking place:

In addition to the **Status** screen, resizing is an event that is captured as well, as shown in the following screenshot:

As I had mentioned previously, when you are looking at the performance-monitoring graphs, you will also (as soon as you use multi-node) see a performance line for the leader node as well as each of the data nodes in your cluster.

If you try to run a query during the resizing operation that in any way changes the data, you will have an error returned, as shown here:

```
ERROR:  Cannot execute query because system is in resize mode
DETAIL:  System is in resize mode, and ONLY read-only queries are allowed to execute.
```

Table maintenance

I know I started off by saying how much maintenance you no longer have to do, and I am not really backing off from that. However, there is still data maintenance that needs to be considered. Since there are no indexes to manage, there really is only the space within the table you need to concern yourself with. The two primary commands are ANALYZE and VACUUM. You can ask my wife; I don't like to vacuum at home, and I don't really like to vacuum my databases, but just like at home, it really is a necessary task. For those of you familiar with Postgres, this is the same command with a different Redshift-specific implementation. Although important, it is not necessarily a lightweight operation, and you should take some consideration to the timing of when you run the vacuum cleaner. However, you don't have to guess when you need to vacuum. There is a system table (svl_vacuum_percentage) that will show you how much space can be reclaimed. If you have relatively small incremental change to the table, such as the result of a daily load, the vacuum will run relativity efficiently. The VACUUM command will reclaim space from a table that has had data movement or deletes. Deletes run incredibly fast in Redshift, as it is simply a logical operation at the time of delete. Do not be alarmed if you have deleted data and you see a difference in a count(*) command from a table that has had data deleted—that is the actual count. If you look in the stv_table_perm system table before the VACUUM command is run, you will get the old (pre-delete) count. The system table has not yet been updated, since the actual rows have not yet been reclaimed. In addition to managing space for the deleted data, the VACUUM command also re-sorts the unsorted parts of the table. Also, when you insert a row based on the sort-key, it is placed in the proper spot on the disk. However, if you update rows, which would change their location within the sorted order, that I/O is delayed until the vacuum is run. The update takes place, and the data is tracked in a special unsorted section of the disk. However, the physical placement of that data in the correct place within the sort-key is what is delayed. The VACUUM command has three options: FULL, SORT ONLY, and DELETE ONLY. The default option, and the one most often used, is FULL. As this implies, it will both reclaim the deleted space as well as re-sort the unsorted parts of the data. There is also the SORT ONLY option, which you can use if you have lots of disk space and need, for query performance reasons, to get the data sorted without taking additional time for reclaiming space. Finally, there is the DELETE ONLY option, which, as the name implies, will only reclaim the deleted space and not re-sort any of the data. This might be useful if you have a very large sort-key and you know you have had a very large effect on the overall table, but not on the order in which the data resides. For the most part, although there are the other options available to you, I don't think you need to do anything other than the default FULL option. If you pick one of the other options, you will likely just be coming back around with the other option, thus having done the work anyway.

There are a few additional system tables that support the VACUUM command:

- SVV_vacuum contains a summary of one row per vacuum transaction, which includes information such as elapsed time and records processed
- SVV_vacuum_progress contains the progress of the current vacuum operations
- STL_vacuum contains the row and block statistics for tables that have just been vacuumed

ANALYZE on the other hand is more about statistical updates and less about physically moving data around in the database. This is a much lighter and less I/O intensive operation. Both of these operations are necessary on a reasonably recurring basis as you are adding data into the database or removing large quantities of data from the database, or if you are performing any operations that affect a large percentage of the rows in a given table. The other option that you have for the ANALYZE command is to run it on a particular column, which particularly on your sort-keys is an important feature. As with most database systems, the better informed the optimizer is, the faster and more consistent your query execution will be. A COPY command will automatically analyze the data after the copy is complete if the data was loaded into an empty table. You can also (optionally) pass the statupdate option to the COPY command, which will cause the analysis of the table after the COPY command has completed. Some columns, which have a lot of change in a given load and which are also used to join to, should be analyzed after each load. Some columns that you will not join to, and most likely will not have in a where clause, will not require analysis as often.

> This command will analyze the whole table: ANALYZE census_data;.
> This command will analyze two specific columns:
> ANALYZE census_data(fips,pop_estimate);.

While we are discussing monitoring table health (with VACUUM and ANALYZE commands), it is logical to take a look at the physical disk as well. While there is less to manage than traditional database management in terms of filegroups, how many physical files, if they should grow or be preallocated, you can still monitor your utilization. There are a few system tables for space monitoring:

- SVV_diskusage is at the block level and contains information about allocation for tables and databases. That is to say there is a row in this system view for every block in the database (that is a large number of rows). Knowing that each is 1 MB in size, you can see how each block is used and the total size of objects with this view.
- STV_partitions contains information about not only usage at the partition level, but also has performance information. There is one row per node and per slice.

Workload Management (WLM)

Workload Management, quite simply, is your ability to control your query environment from a concurrency perspective. If you have worked with Workload Management before in Oracle or the Resource Governor in Microsoft, you may be expecting a bit more control over computing resources. The implementation here is one of queue management for concurrent query execution. I have worked with resource controls in every data warehouse I have ever been involved with; some work better than others; however, without fail, I have been glad that I have taken the time to work through and understand what those utilities brought to each of those environments. My expectation is the same here. It will be worth understanding and setting things up so you have the ability, as best you can, to control queries. There are generally two kinds of queries that run (maybe three) in a data warehouse. The first is from an analyst sitting at a computer with a query window open, making a decision about what he/she wants to look at, and writing/running/fine-tuning/ queries in an interactive and iterative fashion. The second kind of query is one for a defined reporting request. Ideally, this query has been tuned, reviewed, and is asking a well-defined question. It may be a parameter-driven interactive question from a reporting tool, or it could be a scheduled daily/weekly/monthly kind of report. Depending on the utilization, these queries are expected to run between "really fast" and "a few minutes" (these are technical terms for how long queries take). The third kind of query may very well be the scheduled report, or it might be some kind of aggregation or data mining query — the "take longer than you want to wait around for" kind of runtime. Hopefully, your runtime is not really falling into the "it took so long that I forgot it was running" category. You get the idea. These are queries that will churn through a large quantity of data and there is no interactive kind of expectation for the results. The technical runtime length is queries that "take longer than you want to wait around for". Generally, my goal — which I have been able to achieve using the resource allocation tools available within the database — has been to provide a predictable runtime that will match the expectation for the kind of query being run. Predictability is a very important factor. If a report runs for thirty seconds once, and for two minutes thirty seconds the next time, you will be forever disappointing people when the query runs over thirty seconds. You are far better off providing a predictable one-minute runtime than having variability and unrealistic expectations on the "really fast" end of the spectrum. I would never suggest not writing the best possible query to perform the absolute best that it can. This is all relative to the discussion around resource management.

Given the background that I have with successfully implementing these kinds of strategies, naturally I was excited to see that Workload Management (WLM) was provided as part of what Redshift delivers. That sounds like there is a "but" coming, and there is in a way. I really am glad that there is something to control queries; however, whether simply managing concurrency in query queues is a sufficient control to provide the predictable runtimes I am looking for remains to be seen.

The default configuration for a cluster is a single queue that can run five concurrent queries. There is always a queue for the superuser with a concurrency level of 1. This way, you are always guaranteed a slot to run a query (such as killing another query or other administrative tasks). For each queue, you define the concurrency (how many queries get to run together). User groups relate the specific users to groups you assign them to. Query groups are assigned to specific queries at runtime. You can configure a maximum count of fifteen for a combined total for all queues. That does not include the one for the superuser queue that is always there for a given cluster. The limit of fifteen is regardless of the number of nodes or the cluster type. The following diagram shows the hierarchy in the decision-making process of queue assignment. The query will be placed in the first queue that is a match:

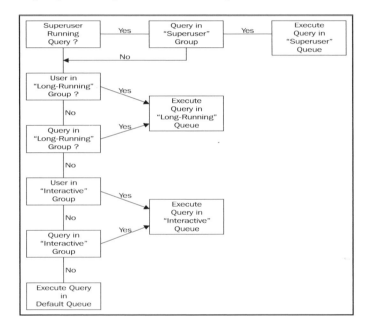

Configuring these queues is a part of the parameter group setup. Select the **Parameter Groups** option, as shown in the next screenshot, from the left-hand side of the Redshift Management console and then select the **WLM** tab:

On that screen, you will see the default configuration of the queues that are set up when you create the cluster, as shown in the next screenshot. As you see with the note on that screen, this default configuration cannot be changed. In order to make changes and set up your own queues, first you must create a parameter group of your own to work with.

To create a parameter group, you will need to pick a name. You can create as many parameter groups as you wish; just keep in mind you can only have one group active at any given time. You may have a need for more than one configuration of WLM queues depending on some kind of event in your business. Switching parameter groups (which we will look at once we create a new one) is similar to resizing something. You will need to plan for this; it is not really a "dynamic" event. There are command-line and API interfaces for the creation and switching of parameter groups, so you can achieve these things programmatically. Regardless of which option you choose to manage your parameter groups, do remember that the group is not immediately applied and a reboot is required. I do recommend coming up with consistent names that you will apply to your user group names as well as your query group names. This will allow you to change parameter groups and the amount of concurrency for a given group without having to change the groups the users and queries are assigned to. Before we go too far into the management of the groups, let's take a quick look at how to create a new parameter group, which is shown in the following screenshot:

You will hopefully be a bit more creative and name the group relative to its intended use with a description of that intent. Once you have your group built, it will be a copy of the default parameter group we have already looked at, the difference being this one you can change. The next screenshot shows you the new parameter group named **parameter-group2**. Select this group and then click on **Edit WLM**:

Once you are in the edit mode, it is a straightforward process of adding queues and reorganizing them to be in the order that you wish them to be processed. Remember that these are going to be processed top-down. The query will be executed in the first group that applies. Additionally, you also cannot create more than a total sum of 15 concurrency values (don't worry, there is a message that will pop up at the bottom of the screen if you allocate more than 15). The configuration that I have created, as shown in the next screenshot, is intended to allow for interactive queries, which (ideally) should be short-running queries that a user is running a selection for to have more allocated slots to prevent those queries from waiting too long in the queue. The long-running queries on the other hand, are not expected to return at "really fast" speeds (a technical term we defined earlier), so those will run longer and wait in queue for a longer time as well. You should also have a catch-all bucket that you cannot actually name as the last queue. This is the default queue. Since the logic that decides which queue has to be applied to run a query in works from the top of the list down, if you get to the last slot and have not defined a user group or a query group, you still want the query to execute. If you pass in a query with a query group name that does not exist, nothing (relative to Workload Management) will happen. The database will simply not act upon it, and when it gets to the end of the WLM list, Redshift will run the query in the default queue.

While we are looking at the creation of our custom parameter group, take a look at the other options that you may want to adjust. The options available to change are shown in the next screenshot. Most likely, the defaults will work for you; however, if you wish, this is where you can make adjustments:

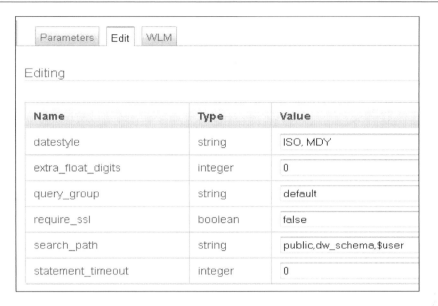

Name	Type	Value
datestyle	string	ISO, MDY
extra_float_digits	integer	0
query_group	string	default
require_ssl	boolean	false
search_path	string	public,dw_schema,$user
statement_timeout	integer	0

As you can see, I chose a different **search_path** option, which we discussed when we looked at creating schemas in the previous chapter. My intent with that change is for user queries to use the public views that I have created, and, if there is no public view, to use the object in the dw_schema schema, and lastly to use the object owned by the user. Beware, this can (and will) cause some confusion for your users. It is important to understand what you are trying to achieve with this change. If it is unclear, you will be very frustrated when you have a table in your own schema and you are not getting the results you expect. Objects will be accessed in the order that they are found in the search path. If there is an object with the same name earlier in the search path, that is the object that will be used.

 Note that there are no options to override the case sensitivity of Redshift. When storing data, "Upper" and "upper" are two different values.

Now that you have the parameter group set up the way you want complete with your Workload Management configurations, you still need to make that parameter group active. Back on the **Cluster Management** page, when you select the **Modify Cluster** option, you will have the option shown in the following screenshot to set which parameter group you want your cluster to run with:

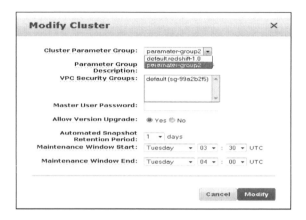

As I mentioned earlier in this chapter, especially for those of you that are familiar with other relational databases, where this sort of configuration is applied online and affects new queries as they come into the engine, which is not the case here. As you will see on your status page (as shown in the next screenshot), Redshift requires a reboot of the cluster for the change of a parameter group to take effect. You can either reboot, or if you wish, simply wait until your next maintenance window appears; the changes will be applied for you at that time. The downside to this is those of you that have configured different groups for different times of the day will need to manage things a little differently. You may consider having a "load" queue; however, since you are limited to a total of 15 concurrency queues, you don't want to slice things too small either.

At query execution time, you have the option of setting the query group you wish to run in a specific query group. If you are a superuser, you can use the superuser group; you may want to utilize that specialized group to run analyze tasks or other maintenance tasks. This will allow your query to execute regardless of how many things are already in queue in the other queues, and also will not take up a slot from some other query.

These next three commands together will run the analyze in the special query group. The first command sets the group, the next runs the analyze, followed by a return to the normal group:

- `set query_group to 'useruser';`
- `analyze census_data;`
- `reset query_group;`

You could analyze the whole database, vacuum, kill a user query, or simply run a regular query. There is no limitation as to what you can run after you set `query_group`; it is simply about picking which queue the query will run in.

Along the same lines, you can assign individual user groups to the query groups for execution. As I discussed when we looked at the creation of user groups for security reasons, it is equally important for management of users and groups to avoid assigning individual users to queues. It is far easier assigning a user to a group that has the proper permissions and then assigning a user to the Workload Management group for proper queue assignment. I would also recommend thinking of your Workload Management groups and security groups as two different things. You can assign permissions to the group that you also use for queue management; however, since the number of queues are limited, and you will likely need to think of them as "Big Queries" and "Small Queries", you will likely have more than two groups for security. Users can be members of more than one group, so create your security matrix and then apply the query queue matrix.

Along the same lines as the other system tables that I have mentioned so far, the following list highlights some of the tables and views available to help you understand, diagnose, and monitor the Workload Management:

- `STL_wlm_error`: Error information
- `STL_wlm_query`: Queries tracked by Workload Management
- `STV_classification_config`: View of the current configuration values
- `STV_wlm_query_queue_state`: View of the current queue status
- `STV_wlm_query_state`: View of the current state of the queries in Workload Management queues

> The more I read abt the #AWS and #Redshift proposition the more I am impressed with the economics. #ovum

Compression

We have been getting progressively more technical as we have been going along, and this section will be no exception. Actually, this part of the book may get a little more technical than what you might think when you hear the term "Getting Started". There is extensive documentation available from Amazon (the links to which are listed in the *Appendix, Reference Materials*), so I will try to keep this at a higher level. If there is a single topic that you should spend time understanding, this may be one of the most important. You will realize that much of the significant gains in performance using the Redshift column store methodology comes directly from the compression of your data in the large 1 MB blocks. The only thing here is that compression is (likely) not what you think it is. If you understand how compression generally works, it is about removal of repeating values and binary storage. This is not that; compression in Redshift is different and more aggressive (particularly with character data). It is more like array processing than anything else. This is where understanding your data in detail will pay off, as it will determine the kinds of gains you will get with each read from the disk. The next screenshot shows the different kinds of compression, the syntax for the CREATE TABLE statement, and the datatypes that are supported by that compression:

Encoding	Keyword in CREATE TABLE syntax	Supported data types
Byte dictionary	BYTEDICT	All except VARCHAR, BOOLEAN
Text255	TEXT255	VARCHAR only
Text32k	TEXT32K	VARCHAR only
Delta	DELTA	SMALLINT, INT, BIGINT, DATE, TIMESTAMP, DECIMAL
	DELTA32K	INT, BIGINT, DATE, TIMESTAMP, DECIMAL
Run-length	RUNLENGTH	All
Mostly*n*	MOSTLY8	SMALLINT, INT, BIGINT, DECIMAL
	MOSTLY16	INT, BIGINT, DECIMAL
	MOSTLY32	BIGINT, DECIMAL
Raw (no compression)	RAW	All

The `Byte dictionary` compression is a method that actually is really more of a removal of redundant values than a compression in the traditional sense. This method works very well if you have a limited number of defined and repeating values. You can have up to 256 unique values. Each physical block on the disk will have a dictionary built (think of it as an array) with an entry for each unique value, then each row has a pointer to the array value rather than storing the unique data. So, in a single byte, you have a pointer to the unique value in the dictionary. You are no longer storing the actual data value, just a pointer. Particularly with long string values with low cardinality, you will be "compressing" those long values to a single byte. This would not work well with a field such as `last_name` as there are far more than 256 unique `last_name` values. However, a field such as `sales_territory` or `state` would be ideal.

The `Text255` and `Text32k` compression works similarly to the `Byte dictionary` compression. Just think of it on a larger scale. There is a dictionary, also at the block level, which will contain an array of the first 245 words in each column (or the first group of words that reach `32K`, if you are using `Text32K`). The array pointer, just as it is in the `Byte dictionary` compression, is then stored rather than the word itself. If you have `varchar` fields that contain multiple words, particularly if there is repetition in those words, you can realize significant savings in each block. You can already begin to see that your understanding of your particular data will be crucial in making the decisions for compression methodologies.

The `Delta` and `Delta32k` encoding will work best with values that can be stored in a sequential order. As the name implies, the values are stored as a delta relative to each other. This is particularly useful for dates, which require a relatively large amount of storage. The first value is stored, and then the next value is stored as the delta difference between the first value and itself, and so on. For a simple example, in 10 records with an integer value of `1` through `10` in the `id` field, the first value would be stored as a 4-byte integer as you would expect, plus a 1-byte flag to indicate the delta compression. The next value is then stored in a single byte as the difference from the previous value, and so on. The only difference between `Delta` and `Delta32` is that `Delta` will store the difference in 1 byte (being able to handle up to 8-bit integers) and `Delta32` will store the difference in 2 bytes (being able to handle up to 16-bit integers).

RUNLENGTH is useful for very repetitive data. The larger the value, and the more repetitive the values are, the greater the compression that will be achieved. This will store the value and the number of times that value is repeated. If the data, even without sorting values, has low cardinality, this may be a good choice. As in the example I cited while explaining the `Byte dictionary` compression, `sales_territory` might be a good choice, as you would have the territory stored, and then the number of additional records that have the same value (the length of the run).

`Mostly` (8/16/32) is about applying a traditional data compression to numeric values, thus storing 8-bit data in 1 byte, 16-bit data in 2 bytes, and 32-bit data in 4 bytes. The difference here is that you can have outliers. If your data type is defined large enough to allow for numbers larger than 8 bytes—however you are mostly storing 8-byte data—you can use the `mostly8` compression. The values that fall outside of the 8 bytes will simply be left as raw data. It is important for these that the data really is "mostly" (more than 80 percent) of the size that you are able to apply the compression to.

> STV_blocklist and STV_tbl_perm that we looked at earlier will help you understand your compression, and will help you know how effective it is.

Now that I have filled your head with all kinds of new information about compression and how you should look at your data, which I believe will provide you the most long term benefit, there are two other options. In the interest of "Getting Started", I believe that the COPY command, especially since you are starting with empty tables, will serve you very well, and get you up and running very quickly. The COPY command that we looked at in the previous chapter for getting your data loaded can automatically analyze and apply compression to the columns at load time based on the data that is being processed. With the `compupdate` option set to `on`, COPY will determine the best possible compression for the data that is being loaded. This option requires that the table be completely empty to start with. The second option is to run analyze compressions against a table that is already populated.

Streaming data

As real-time data warehousing is a topic of discussion at so many companies these days, I thought I would take a break from the highly technical discussions we have been having about the mechanics of running a Redshift cluster and understanding details about how many bytes to store data within 1 MB blocks. This topic is one that is more at the theoretical level, and really will depend on your individual needs, environment, and what kinds of data you have available to you at what frequency. Data warehousing, after all, is really a collection of output from other production systems. Being able to obtain a consistent state from those systems and understanding what data has changed is key to being able to get anywhere close to real time. For example, if the operational database that you are reading from has no timestamps for when data was added or modified, you have little hope of getting to something other than batch processing of tables. Likewise, if there are no message queues or tables that you can read to be informed that data has been altered, real-time data warehousing will be a challenge. You will, in the best case, be able to keep track of some primary key values yourself to determine what data you have read the last time, and also pick up from there if you are sure there are inserts only (such as an e-mail logging table), or you may be relying on a trigger table in the source system to inform you when data has been inserted/updated. If you are familiar with Flume, relative to Hadoop storage, and you were hopeful for that, there is nothing in Redshift that works the same way. In order to achieve real-time data warehousing and stream data from your operational systems, you will need to build processes that are capable of reading, or otherwise be informed of data change that you need to capture in your environment. That is not to say that you cannot build a process that is similar to a Flume process that writes files directly to your S3 bucket, and then a process you have monitoring that bucket directly runs the COPY commands and loads the data as the files become available. Whether it is a direct read of a message queue or a read from files as they are dropped onto S3, there are certainly options that will keep your data latency lower than a 24-hour batch processing cycle. Additionally, if you are already using DynamoDB, the COPY functionality connects directly to that database. You could build processes that would determine which data needs to be sent to the warehouse, and through DynamoDB I would be directly sent to Redshift with a COPY command. Again, most of these decisions will be entirely dependent on your operational system, what kind of architecture you have for those, where the data resides, and how you can be informed of data change that needs to be captured. There are some options that are being developed by a variety of vendors such as Hapyrus, which is developing a product named FlyData that will allow for scheduled movement of data into Redshift.

Query optimizer

The final section of this chapter is to start looking at the query optimizer. We will review execution plans further in the next chapter as we look at querying your data, so for now we will look at things in general terms. The Redshift optimizer, or "query planner", just like most modern-day query optimizers, will go through a number of steps relative to the query that was passed in for execution. Much of the optimization, such as removing unnecessary joins and columns, rewriting correlated subqueries, and so on, is around rewriting the query to obtain the fastest result possible. Don't worry, the optimizer will not change *what* you are asking, just *how* it is being asked. In this case, the optimizer is also aware of the number of nodes in your cluster and the number of slices for a particular table. The optimization process is performed on the leader node, and will actually parallelize the execution request and be compiled into C++ executable code. That code is then passed to each of the data nodes for execution, with the results returned to the leader node. Admittedly, this sounds a lot like map reduce, and the fundamental thought process of distributing work across a cluster to collect data is the same. This is, however, not map reduce. This really is massively parallel database query execution. It is not a scatter gather query, as it might be on a MongoDB cluster, but rather a targeted, optimized query, which, down to the block level, understands where data is located and how it is compressed. Additionally, the query is actually further broken down into executable segments. The optimizer will make adjustments as the query is run to compensate for the kinds of read operations necessary to return the data in the most efficient way. As I said earlier, we will look further at execution plans themselves in the next chapter, as well as the use of the explain plan command. As with any database, the better you can understand the underlying architecture and what is happening when you run a query, the better the chance of architecting a solution that will perform well.

Summary

In this chapter, we once again covered quite a bit of ground. Everything from management functions that you will need to understand to be able to maintain and configure your environment (such as backups and restores), to a detailed understanding of how data is stored at the block-level with compression is covered. You have seen how to resize a cluster as well as how to manage query load using the Workload Management tools. All the while, we have seen how to use the Amazon Redshift Management console to help you with the management functions. We have now got a good understanding of which system tables contain the information you need to help you with the data to support monitoring reports. By this point in the book, you should have a good understanding of what Redshift is, how it works, and what it will take for you to run a cluster. Now that we have covered how to get the data into your cluster and how to manage that data, in the next chapter we will begin to work on querying your data.

5
Querying Data

In this chapter, we will take a closer look at what you need to know to produce results from the data that you have worked so hard to load and organize in the database. We will also take a look at the management of the queries and tools that Redshift provides for understanding the database environment relative to these queries. As far as actual data retrieval goes, there are a few things to think about to optimize performance in the Redshift environment. We have already looked at how compression works, as well as the things you need to consider when creating your table with sort keys and distribution keys. This chapter will look more closely at how to monitor the performance of these tables and understand how to read and understand an explain plan.

SQL syntax considerations

Many of your queries will, if you have implemented the same schema, work with little or no alterations from a syntax perspective. We have already covered, in some detail, the specific things that have not been implemented in Redshift, many of which will not affect the queries running in the database. For clarity within the topic of SQL syntax, I have again listed what I think are some of the more noteworthy items that have not been implemented, which you are most likely to run into with your existing queries:

- String functions: There are really only a couple of string functions you will likely come across that have any kind of regularity (please note that `convert()` and `substr()` are on the list of unsupported functions):

    ◦ `bit_length()`

    ◦ `overlay()`

    ◦ `convert()`

    ◦ `convert_from()`

    ◦ `convert_to()`

- encode()
- format()
- quote_nullable()
- regexp_matches()
- regexp_replace()
- regexp_split_to_array()
- regexp_split_to_table()
- split_part()
- substr()
- translate()

- **Window functions:** Depending on the types of queries you currently have, these may be found in your SQL:
  - row_number()
  - percent_rank()
  - cume_dist()

- These next few items are supported; they are simply things that you should take note of as you look at your current SQL:
  - Some databases allow for spaces in column names, output names, and so on, by placing square brackets ([ ]) around the names that contain spaces. Within Redshift, this is handled with double quotes around the string with the space, for example, "column name".
  - Nulls are treated as they are in most databases within your queries. You can test for IS NULL or IS NOT NULL.
  - As in other databases, you cannot test for equals null as null indicates the absence of data and will not evaluate to equal or not equal as there is no data to test against.
  - Column names are limited to 127 characters and will automatically be truncated if they are no longer without errors.
  - A single table can contain 1,600 columns.
  - Any cluster can contain 9,900 tables.

- As the quote taken from an Amazon Blog about a company testing Redshift states clearly, your queries will likely not be your challenge:

  "We took Amazon Redshift for a test run the moment it was released. It's fast. It's easy. Did I mention it's ridiculously fast? We've been waiting for a suitable data warehouse at big data scale, and ladies and gentlemen it's here. We'll be using it immediately to provide our analysts an alternative to Hadoop. I doubt any of them will want to go back."

Query performance monitoring

Now that you have some of your queries running, you may have built some of the queries that support your end user reporting or even connected your favorite reporting software. One of the challenges that most of us face in any data warehouse environment is "what is running?" When we looked at the implementation of workload management, we discussed the desire to provide a consistent query execution time. Inconsistent query performance, as you know, can be due to other running queries as much as it can be due to the query in question. The Redshift Management console provides quite a bit of good help in the query-monitoring department. Clearly, quite a bit of energy has been spent by Amazon to make query monitoring a seamless and integrated part of the process. Once we review what is available through the Redshift Management console, we will also take a look at the system table that you can use for monitoring. As we in the previous section when we discussed the monitoring of the cluster, start with the **Clusters** option (as shown in the following screenshot) on the left-hand side of the Redshift Management console:

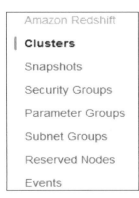

By selecting the performance tab, you will see the importance Amazon has placed on query monitoring as it is at the front and center of Redshift. Basically, you need not worry about query performance and monitoring. The first graph will show you the queries that are executing and the overall length of time. Query monitoring and the relative impact of these queries on system performance is even listed above CPU monitoring, as you can see in the following screenshot:

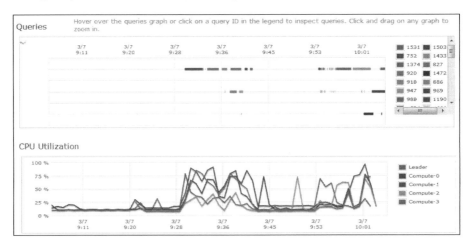

As you hover over one of the graph lines that show the running queries, the right-hand side of the display will change from the query listings to some detailed information as shown in the following screenshot. The details are now about the query, including the actual query text that is running. Too many database systems make it too difficult to get the query that is running. It is refreshing to see that this is so prominent, at the front and center in the monitoring interface, to the point that you almost have to try to avoid seeing what is running.

> Note that if you drag/highlight a selection of the query
> graph with your mouse to highlight a period of time, the
> graph automatically zooms into that level of detail, as do
> all of the other graphs on this page.

When you select the query either by clicking on the query ID from the right of the
graph or by clicking the query ID from the information window when you hovered
over the graph line, either way the drill-down detail provides good information.
The reporting you get for the individual query, just as the cluster reporting, is
broken down into several sections. The CPU utilization and other graphs, when you
look at an individual query, show you the performance of the cluster for the three
minutes before and three minutes after that particular query. This will not only
help you when you are looking at a particular query while it is running but also
provide a fantastic historical context when you are looking back at a query that did
not perform as well as you expected. Understanding the environment that a given
query was running in is key to being able to understand its relationship to the overall
performance of the cluster. The next screenshot shows the CPU graph for the three
minutes before and after the execution of the query that you selected. As you scroll
down in the Redshift Management console from the CPU utilization graph, you will
also find the other graphs we have already discussed (network, disk I/O, and so on);
only now, they are all relative to the time period for this query.

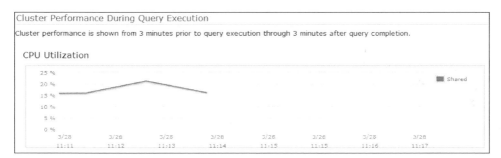

In addition to the performance statistics, you are automatically provided with the explain plan of the query. In my experience, explain plans are too often either an afterthought to building queries or simply something that is a "specialty" task that is left for the database administrator, which is only entertained when there is an issue. This monitoring interface puts the plans in a place where, as you understand the general performance of the system, you will also have a great opportunity to understand what "normal" queries look like. I have long held the belief that there is a science that you can apply for monitoring systems, understanding query behavior, and having expectations for your particular system performance. However, there is a point at which science becomes art. Performance monitoring is not only the application of a science but also a habit. If you are diligent about your monitoring, a single glance at a graph—if you have a good understanding of normal system behavior—should help to tell you when you have a query that you need to go hunt down and figure out. That is not to say you should not set alerts; you should, but you should have a good understanding of what a normal day looks like from a performance perspective.

You may also select the **Queries** tab from the Redshift Management console. As the following screenshot shows, you can select a period of time and see the queries that ran during that period:

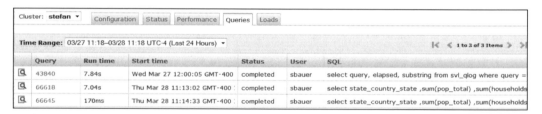

Now that we have looked at the AWS console portion of what is available to monitor your query execution, let's look at some of the system tables that contain the details for you to report on. There are basically three states of a query: waiting, running, and done. These views and tables will give you an insight into query execution, much like the tables and view that we have covered in the earlier chapters. Much of the monitoring that you see in the console is built from these tables:

- STL_query contains high-level information about queries.

- SVL_qlog contains a subset of the information in the STL_query table.

- STL_query_text contains the actual text of the query, 200 characters at a time. Any query that has more than 200 characters will get multiple entries in this table with a sequence number. No DDL has been captured in this table.

- STV_exec_state contains information about the queries that are currently either executing or waiting to execute.

- `STV_inflight` contains information about the queries that are currently executing.

- `SVV_query_inflight` is a view that contains information from the `stv` and `svl` tables. This is a commonly used view of the data.

- `STV_recents` contains current activity and recently run queries.

- `SVV_querystate` contains information about the current state of queries.

- `SVL_query_report` contains detailed information about the query execution, including information about disk and memory utilization at the node level. This is a fantastic resource to find large, resource-intensive queries.

- `SVL_query_summary` contains a higher level of information than the `SVL_query_report` table and is not at the node level. Think of this as the entry point to the query reporting, and then from there you can look at more detail in the `SVL_query_report` table. One of the key things that you will find in the `SVL_query_summary` table is where `is_diskbased='t'`. This field will give you an indication of which queries are unable to be processed entirely by memory.

- `SVL_sessions` contains information about the currently connected sessions. I mention this table here as a way for you to identify the processes that are connected and running. If you are interested in a historical view, the `STL_sessions` table contains the session history.

As you can see from this list of tables, there is quite an array of tools at your disposal, some of which you will use on a daily basis, some of which you will build reports from, and others that are available as diagnostic help when you have issues. There are some large players in the database market that should take note here. There is a lot of value that can be derived from a thorough understanding of queries that have been run on the system and of how they performed. There is nothing proactive that needs to be done within Redshift to capture a query trace or anything else; query execution history, complete with explain plans, is automatic. This will allow you to understand the queries that are running on your cluster; this is very useful if the query you are reviewing is something that someone submitted once and never ran again. You can focus your query-tuning energy on the queries that someone else deployed as part of a scheduled report or another repeating process. It is with these tables that you can understand memory utilization and also get to know the queries that are using the disk I/O.

As you select any of the queries, you will again be presented with the details of the query, the complete query text, and the explain plan for the execution of the query. The next screenshot shows the plan from the query detail; this is a very valuable tool to help determine not only the individual query performance but the overall impact it may have had on other queries.

```
▼ SQL
select state_country_state ,sum(pop_total) ,sum(households) FROM census_data a INNER JOIN all_fips_codes b ON a.fips =
b.fips GROUP BY state_country_state

▼ Explain Plan
XN HashAggregate  (cost=1150200167.74..1150200183.71 rows=3195 width=38)
  ->  XN Hash Join DS_BCAST_INNER  (cost=39.94..1150200143.78 rows=3195 width=38)
        ->  XN Seq Scan on all_fips_codes b  (cost=0.00..31.95 rows=3195 width=31)
        ->  XN Hash  (cost=31.95..31.95 rows=3195 width=25)
              ->  XN Seq Scan on census_data a  (cost=0.00..31.95 rows=3195 width=25)
```

As with most databases, it is very important to be able to understand what you are asking of the database and how it is interpreting that request. The explain plan is your best window into query performance and into identifying if the database is accessing the data in a way that you would expect.

Explain plans

This is another one of those sections that will be a little more technical than most; however, as I have said, reading an explain plan is generally not done by enough people during the development of a query. There is almost always more than one way to ask a question with a query. Understanding how the database engine is reacting to the question is key for a good performance as well as consistently well-written queries.

Understanding the output from the EXPLAIN command is more than simply understanding the order in which the query was processed. It is about understanding the kinds of operators that were used to build the query and how the data was accessed. Through a combination of SVL_query_summary and SVL_query_report data, you can actually map each of the execution steps and understand specific statistics all the way down to memory usage and data distribution. It is important to understand that the EXPLAIN command does not actually run the query. The plan is based on the available statistical data about a table. If you have loaded (or changed) a significant portion of the data in a table, it is possible (probable actually) that you will get different results after you run the ANALYZE command on the table. The other system tables we looked at capture the actual results of the execution based on the plan that was devised by the EXPLAIN command during pre-execution.

```
1     EXPLAIN
   ☐ (select
3         state_country_state
4         ,sum(pop_total)
5         ,sum(households)
6     FROM census_data a
7     INNER JOIN all_fips_codes b
8     ON a.fips = b.fips
9     GROUP BY state_country_state)
```

As I said, the execution of the preceding EXPLAIN command will not execute the query; it will simply return the plan as can be seen in the following screenshot:

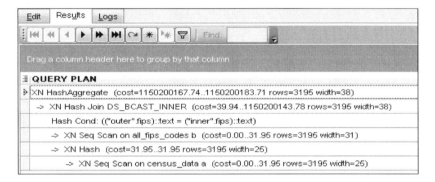

You can also select the explain plan to be displayed in the **EMS Postgres Query Manager** software when you submit the query. You should turn these options on (as seen in the following screenshot). There is no overhead for returning the explain plan. The plan is being generated anyway; you might as well have it returned and begin to understand what the database is doing with each query. There are plenty of ways to see this information, which you will see as we progress through this section. These interactive options, however, will keep the plans at the forefront of your query development.

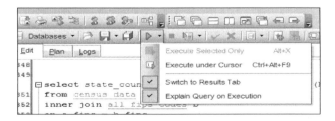

The EMS SQL tool will then return to you the text-based results as well as a graphical representation of the steps in the query, as shown in the following screenshot:

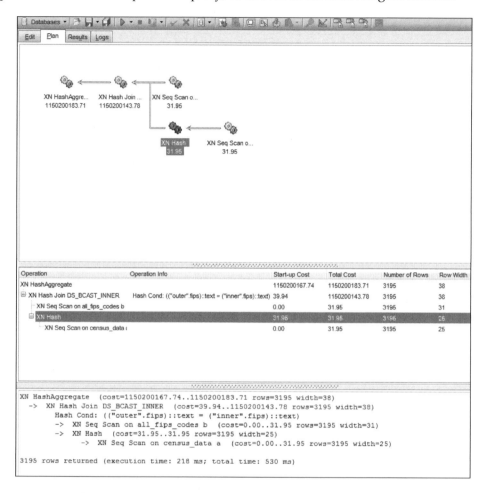

In addition to being able to generate the plan at the time of execution, you can query the STL_explain table (which is what is also displayed on the drill-down for the query performance we just looked at). That data is captured along with the query ID. This allows you to understand the plan that a particular query used after the query runs completely. Regardless of if you are looking at the explain plan as a result of executing the query with the options enabled to capture the explain at runtime or if you are looking at the **Queries** tab in the Redshift Management console, or if you simply executed the command to get the explain without executing the query as we saw earlier, the output produced will be the same. Taking the EXPLAIN command explained earlier, we can take a closer look at what the EXPLAIN command returns in the following screenshot:

Rockbridge County, VA	22307	9291
Sarasota County, FL	379448	169256
Will County, IL	677560	221722
Caldwell County, KY	12984	5047

Grid View   Form View   Print Data

Records fetched: 3195/3195   exec: 218 ms; total

```
XN HashAggregate  (cost=1150200167.74..1150200183.71 rows=3195 width=38)
  ->  XN Hash Join DS_BCAST_INNER  (cost=39.94..1150200143.78 rows=3195 width=38)
        Hash Cond: (("outer".fips)::text = ("inner".fips)::text)
        ->  XN Seq Scan on all_fips_codes b  (cost=0.00..31.95 rows=3195 width=31)
        ->  XN Hash  (cost=31.95..31.95 rows=3195 width=25)
              ->  XN Seq Scan on census_data a  (cost=0.00..31.95 rows=3195 width=25)

3195 rows returned (execution time: 218 ms; total time: 530 ms)
```

In the explain plan, you will see several components:

- **Cost**: This is a cumulative for the query; it is not just for the time a query is going to run but is relative to the query itself. The higher the cost for a part of the plan, the more work the engine expects to do. This is not a percentage, as is represented in other databases, so you can (and will) see numbers greater than 100. This is a numerical representation of how much I/O work is going to be performed by the step. There is a calculation used, as well, for the cost in I/O operations for the CPU time used. In this case, the highest cost factor of the query is the **HashAggregate** operation with a cost of **1150200167.74**. Remember that this is relative to the query itself and is not a measure of the runtime but just of the relative work.

- **Rows**: This is an estimate based on the statistical data provided from the ANALYZE command. In our example, you see that the expected number of rows from the sequential scan is **3195**, and then the grouping is performed with the **HashAggregate** operator with an expected result of **3195** rows.

- **Width**: This denotes how wide the data being processed is. Compression, which we discussed earlier in the book, will have a large impact on the width of the data and on how many rows the database will (expect) be able to read. You will see a different width for each of the parts being processed. This is where understanding your data and what you can apply compression to will pay off.

Remember that query execution is all about expectations. The more information you can provide to the database by way of primary keys or other constraints (remember, they are not enforced) and through a frequent analysis of the tables, the more accurate a decision the optimizer will make about how to execute the query.

I am sure that I have not lost you (yet); however, to really understand the details behind what you see in the explain plan, there is no other way than to get into the details of the most frequently seen operators. There are plenty of other operators, everything from subplans to window functions; however, there are three main processes that just about every query does: **select**, **join**, and **aggregate**. So, I thought I would focus on these three main functions of the query. The Amazon documentation has a significant amount of information on these as well as on many of the other operators you will see in the explain plan.

Sequential scan

One of the most frequent operators that you will find at the bottom of an explain is the sequential scan. This scan operator scans a column (based on your query request). Remember that this is a column store, which has compression applied to the columns, so the scan of a column is not nearly the "big deal" that it is in another database environment. If you are used to reading explain plans in other environments, you will be looking for some kind of index access. Don't (necessarily) worry about the sequential scan operator; you will get more comfortable with this whole process very soon.

Joins

Much of what you will be looking at in the plans will be the kinds of joins that you are getting between the different parts of the query. If you see a nested loop join, be sure to review your query. You likely have some kind of Cartesian product (hopefully on purpose). Your next best choice of a join is the hash join; this is very fast for large data sets—particularly if you are testing for equality when making a comparison to the hash table. As a general rule, the nested loop join will be faster only if the quantity of data is small. Since we are dealing with Redshift and data warehouse side queries, the data that is being processed is generally large. The other join option, which will outperform either of these if you are joining two large tables, is the merge join. This join is best on a column that is used in the sort key as well as on the distribution key for both tables. You will see merge conditions listed in the explain plan as well; this will give you a good idea of how the data is being accessed.

Most of these kinds of operations are things we are all used to seeing in the explain plans of other databases. You may have to adjust your thinking a bit with relation to what they mean and how they apply, particularly in a column store, but the terms themselves should not be too unusual. There are a few new operators that Redshift has added to the mix that relate to how data will be moved around the cluster for processing. As the query will be distributed to the different data nodes for processing, depending on what data is being accessed, data may physically be moved between nodes to satisfy a query. The bottom table in the explain plan output is the inner table. Normally, this table is held in memory and is matched against for filter criteria to limit the data in the larger table.

- ds_bcast_inner: This indicates that the inner table (ideally the dimension) has been broadcast to all the data nodes, so they can all use the data to filter against, without having to bring those parallel streams back together to filter the data. Provided this is not broadcasting the fact table to all the data nodes, this is not a bad thing to see in the explain plan.

- ds_dist_inner: This indicates that the inner table (again ideally the dimension) has been redistributed. This will generally be a portion (slice) of the table and is being aligned with a slice of the table it is being joined with. Think of it as a targeted broadcasting of data. Rather than scattering the data to all the nodes, this moves a portion of the data to better align it with a portion of the other table.

- ds_dist_both: This indicates that portions of both the inner and outer tables are being redistributed so that these slices may participate in the join operation. If you are seeing this consistently, you may want to evaluate the distribution key on the fact table.

- ds_dist_none: This indicates the data is where it needs to be to be joined together and does not need to be redistributed.

It is not possible (nor should you try) to completely eliminate the distribution and broadcasting of data between data nodes. However, if there is a very large amount of consistent data movement, you may want to evaluate how the data is being joined and what is being used for the distribution and sort keys on your tables. It is probably because of these kinds of decisions, and seemingly arbitrary processes, that the art of explain plan analysis has often been left to the DBA. However, with the ease (and regularity) with which you are able to see these plans in Redshift, I hope that you will quickly have the confidence to pinpoint normal query behavior from behavior that needs tuning.

Sorts and aggregations

Many (most) of the queries that are run in a data warehouse environment are used for grouping and sorting something. You will see `HashAggregate` for unsorted and `GroupAggregate` for sorted aggregation functions. One of the most common sort operations that you will encounter in Redshift is the merge operation. This is a result of taking all of the individual parallel operations and bringing them back together into a single result. There is nothing wrong with a merge.

Working with tables

Keeping in mind the location of the data and servers, temporary tables are a powerful tool that can work with intermediate result sets. There are a few options for temporary tables. They can be created either with a traditional `create` statement, with an `into` statement, or with a `create table as` (CTAS) syntax. However, do keep in mind that the `create table as` syntax, regardless of whether it is temporary or permanent, will not carry forward your column-compression encoding. You can use any `create table` statement syntax that normally applies to tables, and by adding the `TEMP` or `TEMPORARY` keyword in the statement, the table will reside in a temporary schema.

Both of these statements will create a table with the same columns as the `all_fips_codes` table:

*   `CREATE TEMPORARY TABLE my_temp_table like(all_fips_codes)`
*   `CREATE TEMP TABLE my_temp_table like (all_fips_codes)`

You may also create a temporary table such as `create temp table all_fips_codes like(all_fips_codes)` that, even for this illustration, is confusing. A temporary table can have the same name as a physical table as it is created in a separate schema. If you remember the discussion about the search path and how you can have multiple objects with similar names, this is no different. The temporary schema that the objects are built in is automatically (you cannot change this) first in the search path. So if you had a reason to create a temporary table with values different from the actual table, you could create it as temporary and load it with values different from the permanent table. Your queries would then be read from the temporary table. The other thing to keep in mind about temporary tables is that they are for the session you are currently in and will disappear when that session ends. There is no concept of global temporary tables in Redshift.

Keep in mind that temporary tables, just like their permanent table counterparts, need to be analyzed for the optimizer to understand the data that is in the table. If you create the table using either `create table as`, `create temp table as`, or `select into`, Redshift will automatically analyze the tables upon creation. In all other methods (such as the `like` method we just looked at) and the methods in which you modify the tables after any give period of time, you should analyze them as you would for any table.

Now that we have looked at creating tables (whether they are permanent or temporary) and at some of the system tables and views to support query monitoring and diagnosis, there are a few more system tables to consider. So far, we have looked at the `STV_`, `STL_`, and `SVV_` prefixed objects, all of which are Redshift-specific tables and views. There is one more group of tables that we have not yet discussed, and these are the native Postgres tables (`PG_`). There is a `PG_` table that will help us look at the physical objects in the database. Although there are a number of these tables available as part of the database schema, some will have data while others will not. If you are familiar with Postgres database environments, this will likely be one of the more foreign things to you as there are tables that you may have relied upon that are simply not used by Redshift; yet, they are still available in the database. The three primary system tables that contain object information are as follows:

- `PG_table_def`: This contains table and column information that you are accustomed to seeing in just about any database

- `STV_tbl_perm`: This contains information about permanent tables; however, although not implied by the name, it also contains information for temporary tables created within a user session

- `STV_locks`: This contains information about current updates on tables

Insert/update

The insert and update activity in Redshift is not all that different from the other databases that you are already familiar with. You can insert data into a table using a SELECT statement or a standard INSERT statement with the VALUES clause to provide the data. The syntax in Redshift to supply a default value to a column during insert is default_expr. It is through the default_expr expression, written at the time that you'll create the column, that you can specify what value you would like to have in the column when no value is provided during the insert. If there is no default_expr value on the column, the value that is loaded to the column is a NULL value. Do note, however, as I have been harping on about the use of views, that you cannot insert, update, or delete from a table though a view. You must access the physical table object directly with those commands. The following screenshot shows the INSERT syntax:

```
INSERT INTO table_name [ ( column [, ...] ) ]
{DEFAULT VALUES |
VALUES ( { expression | DEFAULT } [, ...] )
[, ( { expression | DEFAULT } [, ...] )
[, ...] ] |
query }
```

Updates are handled in the same way that you are accustomed to in other databases. The syntax will alter the data in a table, based on a select statement, or the specific values provided in the SET clause. The following screenshot shows the syntax for UPDATE:

```
UPDATE table_name SET column = { expression | DEFAULT } [, ...]
[ FROM fromlist ]
[ WHERE condition ]
```

Remember, as we discussed earlier when we looked at the management of data with the ANALYZE and VACUUM commands, if you have affected a large amount of data with either an insert or update, it is important to analyze the table as well as vacuum the table to re-sort the data as necessary. Data is never actually altered in place on disk. Updates in Redshift are always handled as delete/append operations.

Now that we have had a look at temporary tables and insert statements, as well as many of the system tables necessary to view objects, let's pull things together with a script that Amazon has published in their developer guide for the analysis of tables (`http://docs.aws.amazon.com/redshift/latest/dg/c_analyzing-table-design.html`). In the following SQL statements, you will see the creation of temporary tables and insert statements, as well as the utilization of a variety of the system tables that we have discussed to gather detailed information about the tables in Redshift:

```
/***********************************
Create a temporary table to hold results
***********************************/
CREATE TEMP TABLE temp_staging_tables_1(
    schemaname TEXT,
    tablename TEXT,
    tableid BIGINT,
    size_in_megabytes BIGINT);

/***********************************
Find the user-tables
***********************************/
INSERT INTO temp_staging_tables_1
SELECT n.nspname,
       c.relname,
       c.oid,
       (
         SELECT COUNT(*)
         FROM STV_BLOCKLIST b
         WHERE b.tbl = c.oid
       )
FROM pg_namespace n,
     pg_class c
WHERE n.oid = c.relnamespace AND
      nspname NOT IN ('pg_catalog', 'pg_toast', 'information_schema')
and
      c.relname <> 'temp_staging_tables_1';

/***********************************
Create a second temporary table for results
***********************************/
CREATE TEMP TABLE temp_staging_tables_2(
    tableid BIGINT,
    min_blocks_per_slice BIGINT,
```

```
    max_blocks_per_slice BIGINT,
    slice_count BIGINT);

/************************************
Collect the block information for all
the tables selected into the first temp.
************************************/
INSERT INTO temp_staging_tables_2
SELECT tableid,
       MIN(c),
       MAX(c),
       COUNT(DISTINCT slice)
FROM (
       SELECT t.tableid,
              slice,
              COUNT(*) AS c
       FROM temp_staging_tables_1 t,
            STV_BLOCKLIST b
       WHERE t.tableid = b.tbl
       GROUP BY t.tableid,
                slice
     )
GROUP BY tableid;

/************************************
Temporary table t report results from
************************************/
CREATE TEMP TABLE temp_tables_report(
    schemaname TEXT,
    tablename TEXT,
    tableid BIGINT,
    size_in_mb BIGINT,
    has_dist_key INT,
    has_sort_key INT,
    has_col_encoding INT,
    pct_skew_across_slices FLOAT,
    pct_slices_populated FLOAT);
```

```
/****************************************
Collect the details for the individual
tables in the two temporary tables.
****************************************/
INSERT INTO temp_tables_report
SELECT t1.*,
CASE WHEN EXISTS (SELECT *
                  FROM pg_attribute a
                  WHERE t1.tableid = a.attrelid
                  AND a.attnum > 0
                  AND NOT a.attisdropped
                  AND a.attisdistkey = 't')
THEN 1 ELSE 0 END,
CASE WHEN EXISTS (SELECT *
                  FROM pg_attribute a
                  WHERE t1.tableid = a.attrelid
                  AND a.attnum > 0
                  AND NOT a.attisdropped
                  AND a.attsortkeyord > 0)
THEN 1 ELSE 0 END,
CASE WHEN EXISTS (SELECT *
                  FROM pg_attribute a
                  WHERE t1.tableid = a.attrelid
                  AND a.attnum > 0
                  AND NOT a.attisdropped
                  AND a.attencodingtype <> 0)
THEN 1 ELSE 0 END,
100 * CAST(t2.max_blocks_per_slice - t2.min_blocks_per_slice AS FLOAT)
/ CASE WHEN (t2.min_blocks_per_slice = 0) THEN 1 ELSE t2.min_blocks_
per_slice END,
CAST(100 * t2.slice_count AS FLOAT) / (SELECT COUNT(*) FROM STV_
SLICES)
FROM temp_staging_tables_1 t1, temp_staging_tables_2 t2
WHERE t1.tableid = t2.tableid;

SELECT *
FROM temp_tables_report
ORDER BY schemaname,
         tablename;a
```

Alter

As the data is stored internally in a column store, a table alter is not a major event. This is where the No-Schema world begins to meet with the schema world. There is still a schema involved in this database, so don't get too excited. However, the "event" of adding additional data into the process is not as complex as it is in most traditional data warehouse implementations. You will still need to perform your normal table maintenance activities to inform the optimizer of the data within the column; however, the alter itself will run very quickly, even on large tables. I am not suggesting that this is a MongoDB data store and that you can simply add something to a table on the fly like you can to a Mongo document. The column store simply makes these alterations to the table structure easier than a traditional RDBMS. It is through the ALTER command that you can rename columns, add columns, drop columns, and add constraints, such as primary keys, to tables. It is important to note, however, that one of the items that we looked at in the unsupported features in *Chapter 2, Transition to Redshift*, is the fact that you cannot alter a column. Once a column is established for a table, the data type, size, encoding, and default values are all set and cannot be changed. The desire to alter a column is another example of where you would want to have your queries utilizing views, as you could create a new copy of a table with a new definition for the column you wish to alter, push the data into the new table, and perform the ANALYZE and VACUUM commands, all without impacting any user queries. Then when you are ready, you can switch the view to the new table, allowing for "background" maintenance to occur.

Summary

In this chapter, we looked at quite a bit of information that goes well beyond simply the question of how to get the data back out of the database. You should have a good understanding at this point of the kinds of things that you will need to look for in your own queries, which may need to be changed before you run them against your Redshift tables. Since the good news is that there is relatively little change, we spent a significant amount of time in this chapter looking at how to understand what is running in your database, and how to understand the performance of queries and their interaction with the other queries that are running at the same time. You have seen the many different ways in which you can view the explain plans for a given query, view the ability to see the plan prior to execution, as a result of the execution, and even be able to look at query history. We looked at the major components of these plans to give you an understanding of the plan and of how it relates to query execution. We closed the chapter with a look at the temporary tables that you will be using to store intermediate results from large queries. Temporary tables will be a tool that will help you to not only understand intermediate results but to also improve the performance of these large queries. In the next chapter, we will take a broader look at some of the topics we have covered in detail throughout the book and provide some general best practices.

6
Best Practices

This chapter will give you some best practices and recommendations that ideally will make your implementation of Redshift a smooth and surprisingly quick process. As part of the best practices for monitoring your cluster, we will also cover the last bit of detail for the book, with information on how to set up automated alerts. By this time, you should have a very good understanding of the architecture and why things work the way they do. We have covered a great deal of information in a relatively short time. The overall goal of this book was to provide you with enough detail to help you make an informed decision, but also, as I said in the beginning, to give you the confidence to give it a try. Had we started the book with something like what you see in the following diagram, you may not have gotten very far.

However, I trust that by this point in the book, the diagram really is self-explanatory and really quite simple. Not only is the diagram understandable, but you also have a high degree of understanding about how Redshift works. You understand what processes are passed to the compute nodes, how queries are broken down into executable code, and what kinds of management functions are available to you for everything from backup/restore to query monitoring.

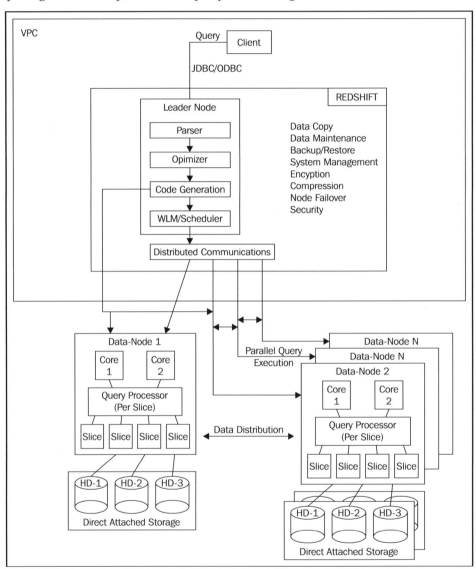

Security

Consider the preceding diagram as a starting point for this discussion. The first thing that you will need with respect to Redshift is access control. The best practice (in general) is to follow the principle of least privilege. Only someone who has a legitimate need should be allowed to access the database, and within this database, they should only have access to the data necessary to perform their job function. Do not allow IPs other than those that are legitimately necessary to access your cluster. Create user groups, assign permissions to these groups, and then associate users with these groups. This will allow you to have users change roles, and as their data access will need to change, their group assignment may change as well. You should have a generic reporting user rather than a specific user established for your automated reports. This will not only allow you to control which workload management queue those queries run in, but you can also ensure that reports will continue to work even if you are to reassign a user to a different security group.

> i just saw a SQL query return a result in < 1min to count 6 months worth of @bitly click data. #tearsofjoy #redshift

Cluster configuration

Single node clusters should only be deployed for testing and development work. There can be no recovery from a node failure (other than from a snapshot restore) if you have a single node. Multiple nodes will not only provide for parallel query and load operations, but will also allow for data protection, as the blocks are replicated between nodes. Additionally, as we have seen, there are some functions that will run only on the leader node. A single node cluster (the leader node) and compute nodes are one and the same, so not only do you fail to gain the benefits of parallel processing, but you actually face the penalty of not having a separate node to handle the tasks of the leader node.

When provisioning your cluster, be sure to pick a maintenance window that will work best for your load times and availability needs. It is also best, particularly early on in Redshift's life cycle, to allow automatic patching for that maintenance window. Notices are published weekly about what is being fixed. In order for these changes to be applied to your cluster, you should allow the automatic patching.

Database maintenance

There are a few notable items for maintaining the tables within the database. Do run the ANALYZE and VACUUM commands on a regular basis, particularly after data has been loaded or updated. The best practice for both of these maintenance commands is to run them without any options (utilizing the default mode of full). Unless there is a particular reason to only reclaim space, or only re-sort data, there is no tremendous saving that will come from delaying these activities. In addition to the routine maintenance of the tables, ensure you have adequate snapshots of your environment. It is always a good idea to take a snapshot just prior to performing a resize activity as well as immediately after the resize activity has completed. This will allow for easy recovery to a pre-resize configuration should something go wrong, as well as recovery to the post-resize configuration. Should you need to restore the database for any reason after the resize, you will have the ability to go back to a known point without having to re-run the resize operation.

Cluster operation

From the topic of database maintenance, we will make a natural transition into the topic of cluster operation. The best practice to back up and restore your cluster is something you should try out and be comfortable with. It is always at the worst possible time that you will really need to have a restore working, so practice this before you need it. Also, remember that restores do not put the cluster into read-only. The cluster is available for use during the restore and will actually prioritize the streaming of the blocks needed to answer query questions. Understanding that is just as important as understanding the fact that a resize operation is a read-only operation, you will not be able to run any update queries. Read-only queries are fine; however, due to the fact that it has an impact on processing, I do not recommend resizing as an elastic response to demand through APIs or command-line operations. Resizing of the cluster should be a planned activity.

Workload Management (WLM) is important to understand. Assigning queries to queues based on the expected complexity (which will generally translate into expected run times) is something you should set up. This can generally be done by assigning specific query tools or products to a given queue. Worry less about the fact that you don't have control over specific resources and focus your attention on overall throughput.

> #Amazon users comparing
> #Redshift to #EMR: "many cases
> of unnecessary usage of
> Hadoop." Interesting discussion:

Database design

The singular best practice in database design considerations is for you to know your data. It is this knowledge that will allow you to make informed decisions on many items that will have a large impact. These impacts can be anything from the amount of storage you will be using (how much you compress your data) to how well queries perform. It is through your unique understanding of the data that you will pick the distribution keys, sort keys, and encoding specifications for compression. When you build tables in your database, provide as much information as possible about each column. Column-level constraints and primary keys are (although not enforced) important for the query planning process to understand what kind of data you expect will be in the table and to make appropriate access decisions. Understanding your data before you create your tables is also important in that the decisions that you make are ones that will live with that table. You can add columns; however, since you cannot change the distribution keys, sort keys, or compression encoding, it is important that you take the time to make decisions that will serve your queries well. Don't rush this step in your analysis in an effort to start running queries.

Sort keys are compound keys that should generally be built with consideration for the order in which the data is naturally being loaded. As many queries will have a recency bias and data will physically be stored on disk in the order that it be loaded, a sort key with a date-time will generally be more helpful than some arbitrary assignment. If you apply a sort key that requires large amounts of data movement within the columns once the data is loaded, the vacuum process will be much more intrusive as it will need to work with a larger percentage of the table. If you are sorting something that is in the natural order of how the data is loaded, the VACUUM command will have less work to do as the data has naturally already been ordered. Whenever possible, match the sort keys between the tables that will often be joined. This will allow merge joins of the sorted columns. Also, do not apply runlength or delta encoding on a sort key column. These very highly compressed encoding schemes may not perform as well when searching for a range of data and then joining that to another table, as those joins will then need to resolve the actual data in order to perform that join.

Distribution keys should be built with slices and nodes in mind. When you decide on your distribution key, it is important to understand what data will most often be queried together and joined in large joins. You do, however, need to understand your data and query practices. If you distribute your data based on a customer key, only one node can possibly be used to answer the question if you are looking at a single customer, and the other nodes will sit idle, which likely is not a good thing. Unless you know that you have an even distribution of queries running for a variety of customers at all times, thereby utilizing multiple nodes, I do not suggest this as a good distribution approach. There is some art to distribution key decisions, as you want to keep large quantities of data together and yet spread the data across the nodes. Although it sounds like it, these are really not opposing goals; multiple nodes working on answering a given question is the goal. Remember that you are dealing with a different kind of storage than you are accustomed to in a standard RDBMS with a column store, and that you are using hardware that was specifically designed to scan large quantities of data very efficiently. You will be better off reading blocks of data on many nodes and eliminating a large percentage of what is returned, rather than getting too granular with your distribution key and not involving enough nodes to answer the query.

> #AWS #Redshift has more compression options than u can shake a stick @

Compression may be the single most powerful tool at your disposal for what will certainly be impressive performance gains. You can rely on the automatic decisions that Redshift will make on your behalf when loading data into a new table. However, as a best practice, I would suggest taking the reins here and making this very important decision for each column. You are going through quite a bit of effort to store and query the data. Providing the best possible results by making compression decisions is important. Do not short change the time to make the correct decisions for your compression encoding.

Private schemas are something you should take advantage of. The best practice for data warehouse design in general is to isolate the physical table structures from your user queries with a layer of views. I have seen too many instances where altering the presentation of data for a specific use was necessary, for everything from the alphabetization of column names (yes, I had that as a requirement) to applying case statements or even calculations. All of these were possible through a view. Imagine having to physically store your data in alphabetical order. Adding columns in the correct order is a maintenance challenge that most of us would not want to entertain.

Monitoring

It should be no surprise to you at this point, given the energy that I already expended on my soap-box about the need to monitor, that I will not be harping on performance monitoring in this section of the book as well. Understanding your overall performance is a very important part of running a data warehouse, regardless of the location of the data. Redshift has made quite a number of tools available to help you understand what is going on in the overall cluster as well as the very specific details down to the individual query level. The best practice for monitoring is to make it a habit. You will have a much better understanding of what is a "good" performance and what is an "unusual" performance if you are diligent about your monitoring routine. The one remaining piece of detail that we need to cover that we have not yet looked at falls within this monitoring category, and that is setting up alarms. I think of alarms as the backstop of monitoring. They are not my primary method of ensuring good performance; however, for off-hour notifications or for other times when the workload increases, alarms provide the mechanism for knowing that there is something that needs to be looked at (ideally before you are notified by someone trying to run a query). The following screenshot shows the section at the bottom of the status screen in the Redshift Management console. In this particular case, no alarms have been configured yet.

To configure a new alarm, select the **Create Alarm** button; this will bring up a dialog window, as seen in the next screenshot, that will define the alarm that you wish to create.

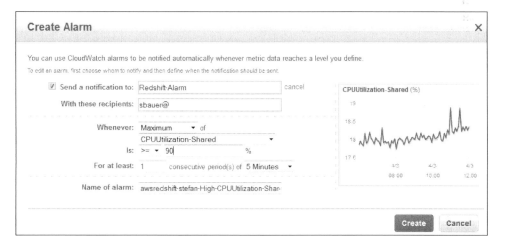

Starting at the top of this screen, you need to pick or define the group that these alerts should go to. You may then pick the kind of threshold you want to measure against (**Minimum**, **Maximum**, **Average**, and so on). You then need to pick the actual event you wish to monitor. The following screenshot shows the different conditions that you can set up monitoring for:

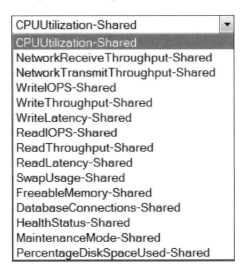

As you can see, there are monitoring items for each of the graphs that we have already reviewed in the performance-monitoring section. You should create (realistic) alarms for each of these. Don't set them at a level that you will ignore when you get the alarm. These should be actionable (or at least important enough for you to go look at what is going on). In an ideal world, you will never get the alarm, but don't assume these are things you don't need to know. In our example, I have selected the **CPUUtilization-Shared** monitor.

You then need to select an operator and a percentage at which you wish to be alerted (**>= 90%**). Once you have that selected, you need to decide how long the monitor should wait before alerting you of an issue. The following screenshot shows the options for how long each interval is. So, if you set **For at least** to **1** and the interval to **15** minutes, the CPU would have to be over a maximum value of 90 percent for more than 15 minutes before the alert was sent.

These configurations should give you a great deal of control over what a "real" alarm is and will allow you to configure these in such a way that you will get a notification for things that matter. Once you have established the alarm, at the bottom of the status page you will see the collection of alarms and their statuses. The following screenshot shows an example of an alarm that is in an **Alarm** state:

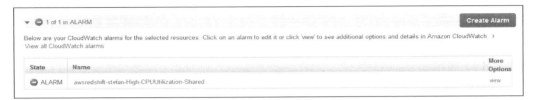

From this screen, you can select the **view** option for that alarm to get the details of what is being reported. The next screenshot shows the details screen. You see the configuration of the alarm, when it was triggered, a graph for that particular condition, and even a **History** tab. Again, Amazon has made performance monitoring something that everyone can (and should) pay attention to.

As you start off with creating alarms, you may want to adjust the individual conditions being monitored. By selecting the **Modify** button at the top of the screen, you will be taken into a step-by-step wizard to modify the alarm. The next screenshot shows the first of these screens, where you can adjust the name, description, as well as the actual threshold. Since you started off by selecting an alarm to work on, you cannot pick a different monitor from here onwards. You are modifying an existing alarm.

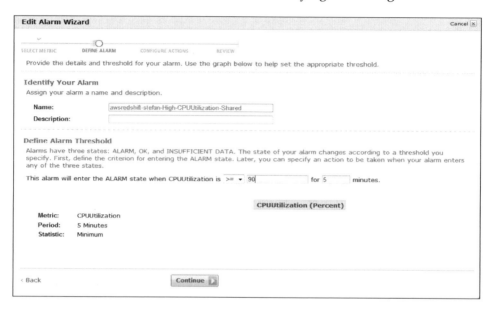

Once you have made the changes to this screen, the **Continue** button will take you to the **Configure Actions** page, as shown in the following screenshot. It is on this page that you can define what group is to be notified when an alarm's condition is met.

The final screen in this wizard is the **Review** screen; here you can verify all of the options that you have selected for the particular alarm. The following screenshot shows the review of the alarm that I have adjusted:

Lastly, when you return to the status screen, at the bottom where you saw the alarm in the **Alarm** condition, you'll now see the same alarm in the next screenshot with the all-clear **OK** status:

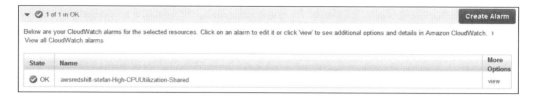

To close the discussion on monitoring, it is equally important to understand the activity in the database at the individual query level and to understand what each query is doing. Do not shy away from explain plans, and help your users understand how to read them also. There is valuable information in the plans. Some knowledge of these plans will tend to take the intimidation of reading them away. As you review plans, also consider temporary tables for managing intermediate data sets. No data warehouse database is a "set it and forget it" kind of environment. Understand that data volumes change, query patterns change, and new data sources are always added. Continual habitual monitoring is key to providing an environment that will live up to your users' expectations. Also, as you are monitoring and benchmarking query executions, remember that you should run a query twice to get a benchmark time. The initial query execution will have an overhead associated with code generation that should not factor into your benchmark times.

Data processing

Redshift is a batch-oriented environment optimized to perform large data loads utilizing the COPY command. That is not to say that you cannot get something approaching "real time", as we discussed earlier in the book. However, you do need to keep in mind all of the work that is going into the distribution and replication of the underlying data for each transaction you are committing. In addition to this, keep in mind that Redshift will never modify data in-place. Updates will actually delete the data and insert a new row with the updated data. It is best to perform bulk operations with the COPY command whenever possible.

The COPY command will load data in parallel. Take advantage of this by splitting your files into parts in a directory on your S3 bucket. It is best to initiate the copy for the directory that contains multiple files to allow for parallel loading of the data. Any data that has not yet been successfully stored or arrives after your copy is initiated will not be copied. If you are using the COPY command from DynamoDB, it is best to time-shift the data within that database (for example, by hour), then initiate the copy from the time-shifted tables.

Summary

This chapter tied together some of the loose ends from the topics that we covered earlier in the book. In *Appendix, Reference Materials*, you will find reference materials for the details that we covered together with the links to Amazon documentation and other useful resources of the Redshift technology. It is with the thought of how to apply this technology, and why you should consider the direction of your data storage in general, that I conclude this book. Storage technology and specific databases will not solve your business problems. The following Twitter quote about where the analysts will come from is a very real-world problem and has nothing to do with the underlying technology:

> Finally! Math is "in". Netflix bases bet on #bigdata, but where will the analysts come from?

As I wrote this final chapter, it crossed my mind how few explanations of terms and details related to the functionality of the database I had to get into. It is my hope that through this relatively short journey of *Getting Started with Redshift*, you have gained a true understanding of how this database functions. I feel that regardless of your interest in the Redshift product, at this point you should be able to have a clear and intelligent conversation about this product's capabilities with just about anyone. As far as the larger topic currently brewing in the industry, I will leave it to you to how to exactly define "big data". However, if big data for your environment is 2 terabytes or 1.6 petabytes, Redshift's ability to scale will serve you well as your data grows. As more and more companies take the "no data left behind" approach, your data universe, without any question, will continue to expand. The thing that is obvious — as more and more data is produced and the rate of data growth continues to geometrically escalate — is to have a scalable solution for your data needs, which will be key as you look towards the future. It is clear that it is not only the data warehousing software vendors, with the rapid adoption of ETL products for Redshift, but also the Business Intelligence software vendors that have taken notice of this fact. The list of Redshift partners is growing quickly; this will ultimately lead to an even higher adoption rate than what is already being seen. Throughout the book, there have been seemingly random Twitter quotes from people about Redshift, its performance, and about big data topics in general. These quotes are not a scientific measure of any experiences, but just serve as a reminder that the big data topic is one of daily discussion.

There are very few companies that are not, in some form or another, taking notice of cloud storage, big data, and what it means to gain an understanding from the large amounts of information being generated by absolutely every industry.

> The more I read abt the #AWS and #Redshift proposition the more I am impressed with the economics. #ovum

Every business is trying to get a competitive edge over others in their market by understanding customer behavior, the interaction of seemingly unrelated events, and every other imaginable combination. It is through these analyses that businesses will better understand and target their investments. Redshift will allow you the scalability and ease of management that will allow you to focus your energy on helping analysts understand the vast new data world that you are storing for them. Your analysts will appreciate the ease of use and immediate comfort they will have as they can use the tools and methodologies they are already familiar with.

So, as your data grows and your analytical needs grow as well, consider Redshift as you make decisions about how and where to store your data. There is likely no single answer to what is "right"; however, Redshift is a powerful and affordable option to have available to you as you make these decisions.

Reference Materials

This section of the book is intended as a quick reference containing some of the commands and terms that were covered throughout the other chapters.

Cluster terminology

Here is a detailed list of cluster terminologies that you should be aware of:

- **Application Programming Interface (API)**: We looked at some of the available API calls in *Chapter 2, Transition to Redshift*. There is extensive API documentation available at `http://docs.aws.amazon.com/redshift/latest/APIReference/Welcome.html`.

- **aws_access_key**: Your public key from the ID you have from Amazon's AMI (explained further down this list) that allows you access to the Redshift Management console.

- **asw_secret_access_key**: The private part of your access key. The combination of the public and private parts will identify you to Amazon services.

- **Block**: The physical storage unit for the data on disk; Redshift stores data in 1 MB blocks.

- **Cluster**: The collection of nodes with a Redshift instance.

- **Cluster snapshot**: The backup/restore methodology (see *Chapter 4, Managing Your Data*).

- **Column store**: The method of storing data in columns rather than in rows.

- **Command line**: The Amazon command-line interface, which allows for cluster management (see *Chapter 2, Transition to Redshift*). Here are some useful links:
    - `http://aws.amazon.com/cli/`
    - `http://docs.aws.amazon.com/redshift/latest/cli/welcome.html`

- **Compression**: The methodology applied to the data to reduce the physical storage size and increase read performance (see *Chapter 4, Managing Your Data*).

- **Data node** (also known as the compute node): This stores the distributed data for the cluster and executes (compiled code) queries returning data to the leader node.

- **Distribution key**: A single column, chosen at the time of table creation, that will control the physical distribution of data among nodes (see *Chapter 3, Loading Your Data to Redshift*).

  ○ **ds_bcast_inner**: The execution plan description that indicates that the inner table has been broadcast to all data nodes (see *Chapter 5, Querying Data*).

  ○ **ds_dist_both**: The execution plan description that indicates that portions of both the inner and outer table are being redistributed (see *Chapter 5, Querying Data*).

  ○ **ds_dist_inner**: The execution plan description that indicates that the inner table has been redistributed (see *Chapter 5, Querying Data*).

  ○ **ds_dist_none**: The execution plan description that indicates the data is where it needs to be to join together and does not need to be redistributed (see *Chapter 5, Querying Data*).

- **EC2**: Instances of Linux machines. These machines can be used to host other software, your own scripting tasks, and so on (we looked at command-line configuration in *Chapter 2, Transition to Redshift*).

- **Encryption**: Allows for secure storage of data utilizing a private key that is never persisted on disk within the Redshift environment. The key is stored on the control network behind firewalls and is moved into Redshift memory on startup of the instance.

- **Explain plan**: The output from the query optimization process showing the access path, joins, and the cost for a particular query.

- **Identity and Access Management (AMI)**: Amazon's method for establishing user accounts and what those accounts have access to. See the Amazon administrator at your site to get a user ID that has access to Redshift services.

- **Leader node**: The node responsible for primary management of the cluster. It manages inbound and outbound data as well as certain "leader only" data functions that are not distributed to other nodes.

- **Parameter group**: The collection of default cluster settings (such as data format) as well as the Workload Management settings.

- **Query planner**: The Redshift query optimization engine.

- **Redshift Management console**: A web-based management console for managing and monitoring your Redshift clusters.

- **Resize**: The allocation of more (or fewer) computing resources to your cluster (see *Chapter 4, Managing Your Data*).

- **Search path**: The order in which schemas are searched for in objects. Adjustable in the parameter group settings.

- **Slice**: Each data node will have a number of slices for a given table, one for each of the the CPUs.

- **Sort key**: The compound key established at the time a table is created to physically order the data on disk (see *Chapter 3, Loading Your Data to Redshift*).

- **S3**: The Amazon file storage system.

- **Virtual Private Cloud (VPC)**: This is optional in the configuration for Redshift, however, Redshift will run within a VPC.

- **Workload Management (WLM)**: The management of concurrency within the cluster (we looked at how to configure WLM in *Chapter 4, Managing Your Data*).

Compression

Chapter 4, Managing Your Data, covers the usage of the different compression encoding types used in Redshift. The following table lists the available encoding types and the associated datatypes that are supported:

Encoding	Keyword in CREATE TABLE syntax	Supported data types
Byte dictionary	BYTEDICT	All except VARCHAR, BOOLEAN
Text255	TEXT255	VARCHAR only
Text32k	TEXT32K	VARCHAR only
Delta	DELTA	SMALLINT, INT, BIGINT, DATE, TIMESTAMP, DECIMAL
	DELTA32K	INT, BIGINT, DATE, TIMESTAMP, DECIMAL
Run-length	RUNLENGTH	All
Mostly*n*	MOSTLY8	SMALLINT, INT, BIGINT, DECIMAL
	MOSTLY16	INT, BIGINT, DECIMAL
	MOSTLY32	BIGINT, DECIMAL
Raw (no compression)	RAW	All

Datatypes

In *Chapter 4, Managing Your Data*, we looked at some datatypes for compression encoding. Also, in *Chapter 2, Transition to Redshift*, we looked at the SQL data types.

The following are the allowable datatypes and their aliases:

Data type	Aliases	Description
SMALLINT	INT2	Signed two-byte integer
INTEGER	INT, INT4	Signed four-byte integer
BIGINT	INT8	Signed eight-byte integer
DECIMAL	NUMERIC	Exact numeric of selectable precision
REAL	FLOAT4	Single precision floating-point number
DOUBLE PRECISION	FLOAT8	Double precision floating-point number
BOOLEAN	BOOL	Logical Boolean (true/false)
CHAR	CHARACTER	Fixed-length character string
VARCHAR	CHARACTER VARYING	Variable-length character string with a user-defined limit
DATE		Calendar date (year, month, day)
TIMESTAMP		Date and time (without time zone)

Here is the list for integer ranges and sizes:

Name	Storage	Range
SMALLINT or INT2	2 bytes	-32768 to +32767
INTEGER, INT, or INT4	4 bytes	-2147483648 to +2147483647
BIGINT or INT8	8 bytes	-9223372036854775807 to 9223372036854775807

Here is the list for decimal precision and sizes:

Name	Storage	Range
REAL or FLOAT4	4 bytes	6 significant digits of precision
DOUBLE PRECISION, FLOAT8, or FLOAT	8 bytes	15 significant digits of precision

SQL commands

The SQL commands listed here are either different from standard SQL implementations due to Redshift needs or are otherwise important to highlight. This is not a SQL reference; most SQL that you will run in Redshift will function as you would expect it to normally.

- **ALTER**: This command is at the table level only; there are no alter column commands (see *Chapter 5, Querying Data*).

- **ANALYZE**: The command used to capture statistical information about a table for use by the query planner (see *Chapter 4, Managing Your Data*).

- **COPY**: The following screenshot shows the syntax of this command (see *Chapter 3, Loading Your Data to Redshift*):

```
COPY table_name [ (column1 [,column2, ...]) ]
FROM 's3://objectpath'
[ WITH ] CREDENTIALS [AS] 'aws_access_credentials'
[ option [ ... ] ]

where option is

{ DELIMITER [ AS ] 'delimiter_char'
| FIXEDWIDTH 'fixedwidth_spec' }
| ENCRYPTED
| GZIP
| REMOVEQUOTES
| EXPLICIT_IDS
| MAXERROR [ AS ] error_count
| DATEFORMAT [ AS ] 'dateformat_string'
| TIMEFORMAT [ AS ] 'timeformat_string'
| IGNOREHEADER [ AS ] number_rows
| ACCEPTANYDATE
| IGNOREBLANKLINES
| TRUNCATECOLUMNS
| FILLRECORD
| TRIMBLANKS
| NOLOAD
| NULL [ AS ] 'null_string'
| EMPTYASNULL
| BLANKSASNULL
| COMPROWS numrows
| COMPUPDATE [ { ON | TRUE} | { OFF | FALSE } ]
| STATUPDATE [ { ON | TRUE} | { OFF | FALSE } ]
| ESCAPE
| ROUNDEC
```

- **CREATE TABLE**: Here is a command reference for this SQL statement (see *Chapter 3, Loading Your Data to Redshift*):

```
CREATE [ [LOCAL ] { TEMPORARY | TEMP } ]
TABLE table_name
(
{column_name data_type
[ DEFAULT default_expr ]
[ IDENTITY ( seed, step) ]
[ column_constraint ]
[ ENCODE encoding ]
[ DISTKEY ]
[ SORTKEY ]
| table_constraint
| LIKE parent_table
[ { INCLUDING | EXCLUDING } DEFAULTS ] } [, ... ]
)
[ DISTSTYLE { EVEN | KEY } ]
[ DISTKEY ( column_name ) ]
[ SORTKEY ( column_name [, ...] ) ]

where column_constraint is:

[ CONSTRAINT constraint_name ]

{ NOT NULL |
NULL |
UNIQUE |
PRIMARY KEY |
REFERENCES reftable
[ ( refcolumn ) ]}

and table_constraint is:

[ CONSTRAINT constraint_name ]
{ UNIQUE ( column_name [, ... ] )  |
PRIMARY KEY ( column_name [, ... ] ) |
FOREIGN KEY (column_name [, ... ] )
REFERENCES  reftable
[ ( refcolumn ) ]}
```

- **GRANT**: Used to allow specific permissions to an object or schema. The syntax is GRANT [permission] on [object] to [username].

- **CREATE GROUP**: Used to associate users to a logical grouping. The syntax is CREATE GROUP group_name [[with] [USER username(s)]].

- **CREATE SCHEMA**: Used to isolate objects. The syntax is CREATE SCHEMA schema_name [AUTHORIAZATION username] [schema_element(s)].

- **VACUUM**: A process to physically reorganize tables after load activity (see *Chapter 4, Managing Your Data*).

System tables

The following is a detailed list of the system tables used in Redshift:

- **PG_**: The prefix for Postgres system tables and persistent storage. It is mostly used only to store information about objects. Most other system tables are Redshift-specific tables.
- **STL_**: The prefix for Redshift system tables and persistent storage.
- **STV_**: The prefix for the Redshift system virtual table view; it contains current data for the cluster.
- **SVV_**: The prefix for the Redshift system view; it contains stored queries and views that combine both STL_ and STV_ tables and views.
    - ○ **PG_table_def**: The table that contains column information
    - ○ **STV_blocklist**: The view of the current block utilization
    - ○ **STV_tbl_perm**: The view of the current table objects
    - ○ **STV_classification_config**: The view of the current configuration values
    - ○ **STV_exec_state**: The view that contains information about the queries that are currently being executed or are waiting to be executed
- **SVV_diskusage**: This view is at the block level and contains information about allocation for tables and databases.
- **STV_inflight**: This view contains information about the queries that are currently being executed.
- **STV_partitions**: This view does not only contain information about usage at the partition level but also has performance information. There is one row per node, per slice.
- **STL_file_scan**: This table contains information about which files on which nodes were accessed during the data copy operation.
- **STL_load_commits**: This table contains information about which query, which filename, how many rows, and which slice were affected by a load.
- **STL_load_errors**: This table contains information about the particular error that was encountered during the load.
- **STL_load_error_detail**: This table contains detailed data for any error that you encounter and find in the STL_load_errors table.
- **STV_load_state**: This view contains the current state of the copy commands, including the percentage of completed data loads.

- **STV_locks**: This view contains information about current updates on tables.
- **STL_tr_conflict**: This table contains information about errors involving locking issues.
- **SVL_qlog**: This view contains a subset of the information contained in the `STL_query` table.
- **STL_query**: This table contains high-level information about queries. The following views are derived from this table:
    - **SVV_query_inflight**: This view contains information from the `stv` and `svl` tables. This is a commonly used view of the data.
    - **SVL_query_report**: This view contains detailed information about query execution, including information about disk and memory utilization at the node level.
    - **SVV_querystate**: This view contains information about the current state of queries.
- **STL_query_text**: This table contains the actual text of the query, 200 characters at a time.
    - **SVL_query_summary**: This view contains a higher level of information than the detail query tables.
    - **STV_recents**: This view contains the current activity and recently run queries.
    - **SVL_sessions**: This view contains information about the currently connected sessions.
    - **STV_tbl_perm**: This view contains information about permanent (and temporary) tables.
- **STL_vacuum**: This table contains row and block statistics for tables that have just been vacuumed.
- **SVV_vacuum**: This view contains a summary of one row per vacuum transaction, which includes information such as elapsed time and records processed.
- **SVV_vacuum_progress**: This view contains the progress of the current vacuum operations.
- **STL_wlm_error**: This table contains Workload Management error information.
- **STL_wlm_query**: This table contains queries tracked by Workload Management.
- **STV_wlm_query_queue_state**: This view contains the current queue status.
- **STV_wlm_query_state**: This view contains the current state of the queries in Workload Management queues.

Third-party tools and software

The following are links to the external software, products, documentation, and datafiles discussed in various sections of the book:

- **Amazon Redshift documentation**: `http://aws.amazon.com/documentation/redshift/`

- **Amazon Redshift partners**: `http://aws.amazon.com/redshift/partners/`

- **Client JDBC drivers**: `http://jdbc.postgresql.org/download/postgresql-8.4-703.jdbc4.jar`

- **Client ODBC drivers**:

    For 32 bit, use `http://ftp.postgresql.org/pub/odbc/versions/msi/psqlodbc_08_04_0200.zip`

    For 64 bit, use `http://ftp.postgresql.org/pub/odbc/versions/msi/psqlodbc_09_00_0101-x64.zip`

- **Cloudberry Explorer – Amazon S3 file management utility**: `http://www.cloudberrylab.com/free-amazon-s3-explorer-cloudfront-IAM.aspx`

- **The EMS software (SQL Manager Lite)**: `http://www.sqlmanager.net/products/postgresql/manager`

    This is my query tool of choice, as I explained in *Chapter 2, Transition to Redshift*

- **Hapyrus**: `http://www.hapyrus.com/`

    Hapyrus (`http://www.pentaho.com/`) developed a product called **FlyData** to move data to Redshift Pentaho, a type of ETL/BI software

- **Perl**: This scripting language, often used for file manipulation, is used in examples explained in *Chapter 3, Loading Your Data to Redshift* (for more information, see `http://www.activestate.com/activeperl`)

- **Python**: The Python (`www.python.org`) interpreter is needed to run the command-line interface

- **SQL Workbench/J**: A query tool recommended by Amazon; find it at `http://www.sql-workbench.net/`

- **S3 Fox**: The Amazon S3 file management utility (`http://www.s3fox.net/`)

- **United States Census Data**: Contains downloads for *Chapter 3, Loading Your Data to Redshift* datafiles (`http://quickfacts.census.gov/qfd/download_data.html`)

Index

G

general options, PSQL command line 37
GRANT command 128
GroupAggregate 100

H

Hapyrus
  about 58, 131
  URL 131
HashAggregate 100
Hbase 58
High Storage Eight Extra Large
    (8XL) DW Node 9
High Storage Extra Large (XL) DW Node 9

I

Identity and Access Management
    (IAM) 15, 124
indexing strategies 62
Informatica 58
insert and update activity 102
INSERT statement 102

J

joins 98, 99

L

leader node 124
load troubleshooting 54, 55

O

on-demand pricing 9
output format options,
    PSQL command line 36
overlay() method 87

P

parameter group 21, 124
Pentaho 28, 58
percent_rank() method 88
performance monitoring 59-61, 115-120

Perl

Perl
  about 131
  URL 131
PG_ prefix 129
PG_table_def table 101, 129
PowerCenter product 28
pricing 9
PSQL command line
  about 36
  API functions 37
  connection options 36
  general options 37
  output format options 36
Python
  about 33, 131
  URL 131

Q

query optimizer 86
query performance monitoring 89-93
query planner 124
query tools 27, 28
quote_nullable() method 88

R

recovery 66-68
Redgate 66
Redshift
  about 8, 109
  best practices 109
  configuration options 10, 11
  datatypes 40, 41, 126
  system tables 129, 130
Redshift Management console 125
regexp_matches() method 88
regexp_replace() method 88
regexp_split_to_array() method 88
regexp_split_to_table() method 88
reserved pricing 9
resize 125 69-71
Rman 66
row_number() method 88

Thank you for buying
Getting Started with Amazon Redshift

About Packt Publishing

Packt, pronounced 'packed', published its first book "Mastering phpMyAdmin for Effective MySQL Management" in April 2004 and subsequently continued to specialize in publishing highly focused books on specific technologies and solutions.

Our books and publications share the experiences of your fellow IT professionals in adapting and customizing today's systems, applications, and frameworks. Our solution based books give you the knowledge and power to customize the software and technologies you're using to get the job done. Packt books are more specific and less general than the IT books you have seen in the past. Our unique business model allows us to bring you more focused information, giving you more of what you need to know, and less of what you don't.

Packt is a modern, yet unique publishing company, which focuses on producing quality, cutting-edge books for communities of developers, administrators, and newbies alike. For more information, please visit our website: www.packtpub.com.

About Packt Enterprise

In 2010, Packt launched two new brands, Packt Enterprise and Packt Open Source, in order to continue its focus on specialization. This book is part of the Packt Enterprise brand, home to books published on enterprise software – software created by major vendors, including (but not limited to) IBM, Microsoft and Oracle, often for use in other corporations. Its titles will offer information relevant to a range of users of this software, including administrators, developers, architects, and end users.

Writing for Packt

We welcome all inquiries from people who are interested in authoring. Book proposals should be sent to author@packtpub.com. If your book idea is still at an early stage and you would like to discuss it first before writing a formal book proposal, contact us; one of our commissioning editors will get in touch with you.

We're not just looking for published authors; if you have strong technical skills but no writing experience, our experienced editors can help you develop a writing career, or simply get some additional reward for your expertise.

IBM Websphere Portal 8: Web Experience Factory and the Cloud

ISBN: 978-1-849684-04-0   Paperback: 474 pages

Build a comprehensive web portal for your company with a complete coverage of all the project lifecycle stages

1. The only book that explains the various phases in a complete portal project life cycle

2. Full of illustrations, diagrams, and tips with clear step-by-step instructions and real time examples

3. Take a deep dive into Portal architectural analysis, design and deployment

Amazon SimpleDB Developer Guide

ISBN: 978-1-847197-34-4   Paperback: 252 pages

Scale your application's database on the cloud using Amazon SimpleDB

1. Offload the time, effort, and capital associated with architecting and operating a simple, flexible, and scalable web database

2. A complete guide that covers everything from installation to advanced features aimed at optimizing your application

3. Examine SimpleDB and the relational database model and review the Simple DB data model

Please check **www.PacktPub.com** for information on our titles

Amazon Web Services: Migrating your .NET Enterprise Application

Evaluate your Cloud requirements and successfully migrate your .NET Enterprise application to the Amazon Web Services Platform

Rob Linton

Amazon Web Services: Migrating your .NET Enterprise Application

ISBN: 978-1-849681-94-0   Paperback: 336 pages

Evaluate your Cloud requirements and successfully migrate your .NET Enterprise application to Amazon Web Services Platform

1. Get to grips with Amazon Web Services from a Microsoft Enterprise .NET viewpoint

2. Fully understand all of the AWS products including EC2, EBS, and S3

3. Quickly set up your account and manage application security

Quick answers to common problems

OpenStack Cloud Computing Cookbook

Over 100 recipes to successfully set up and manage your OpenStack cloud environments with complete coverage of Nova, Swift, Keystone, Glance, and Horizon

Kevin Jackson

OpenStack Cloud Computing Cookbook

ISBN: 978-1-849517-32-4   Paperback: 444 pages

Over 100 recipes to successfully set up and manage your OpenStack cloud environments with complete coverage of Nova, Swift, Keystone, Glance and Horizon

1. Learn how to install and configure all the core components of OpenStack to run an environment that can be managed and operated just like AWS or Rackspace

2. Master the complete private cloud stack from scaling out compute resources to managing swift services for highly redundant, highly available storage

3. Practical, real world examples of each service are built upon in each chapter allowing you to progress with the confidence that they will work in your own environments

Please check **www.PacktPub.com** for information on our titles

8856779R00086

Printed in Great Britain
by Amazon.co.uk, Ltd.,
Marston Gate.